THE PALESTINIANS

Modern Middle East Nations
AND THEIR STRATEGIC PLACE IN THE WORLD

THE PALESTINIANS

ANNA CAREW-MILLER

MASON CREST PUBLISHERS
PHILADELPHIA

Produced by OTTN Publishing, Stockton, New Jersey

Mason Crest Publishers
370 Reed Road
Broomall, PA 19008
www.masoncrest.com

First printing

1 3 5 7 9 8 6 4 2

Library of Congress Cataloging-in-Publication Data

Carew-Miller, Anna.
The Palestinians / Anna Carew-Miller.
p. cm. — (Modern Middle East nations and their strategic place in the world)
Summary: Discusses the geography, history, economy, government, religion, people, foreign
relations, and major cities of the Palestinians.
Includes bibliographical references and index.
   ISBN 1-59084-513-7
1. Palestine—Juvenile literature. 2. Palestinian Arabs—Juvenile literature.   [1. Palestine. 2.
Palestinian Arabs.]   I. Title. II. Series.
DS118.C225 2003 956.95'3—dc21

                              2002013010

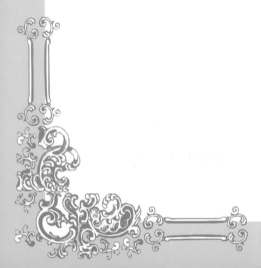

Modern Middle East Nations
AND THEIR STRATEGIC PLACE IN THE WORLD

TABLE OF CONTENTS

Modern Middle East Nations
AND THEIR STRATEGIC PLACE IN THE WORLD

Dr. Harvey Sicherman, president and director of the Foreign Policy Research Institute, is the author of such books as *America the Vulnerable: Our Military Problems and How to Fix Them* (2002) and *Palestinian Autonomy, Self-Government and Peace* (1993).

Introduction

by Dr. Harvey Sicherman

Situated as it is between Africa, Europe, and the Far East, the Middle East has played a unique role in world history. Often described as the birthplace of religions (notably Judaism, Christianity, and Islam) and the cradle of civilizations (Egypt, Mesopotamia, Persia), this region and its peoples have given humanity some of its most precious possessions. At the same time, the Middle East has had more than its share of conflicts. The area is strewn with the ruins of fortifications and the cemeteries of combatants, not to speak of modern arsenals for war.

Today, more than ever, Americans are aware that events in the Middle East can affect our security and prosperity. The United States has a considerable military, political, and economic presence throughout much of the region. Developments there regularly find their way onto the front pages of our newspapers and the screens of our television sets.

Still, it is fair to say that most Middle Eastern countries remain a mystery, their cultures and religions barely known, their peoples and politics confusing and strange. The purpose of this book series is to change that, to educate the reader in the basic facts about the 23 states and many peoples that make up the region. (For our purpose, the Middle East also includes the North African states linked by ethnicity, language, and religion to the Arabs, as well as Somalia and Mauritania, which are African but share the Muslim religion and are members of the Arab League.) A notable feature of the series is the integration of geography, demography, and history; economics and politics; culture and religion. The careful student will learn much that he or she needs to know about ever so important lands.

A few general observations are in order as an introduction to the subject matter.

The first has to do with history and politics. The modern Middle East is full of ancient sites and peoples who trace their lineage and literature to antiquity. Many commentators also attribute the Middle East's political conflicts to grievances and rivalries from the distant past. While history is often invoked, the truth is that the modern Middle East political system dates only from the 1920s and was largely created by the British and the French, the victors of World War I. Such states as Algeria, Iraq, Israel, Jordan, Kuwait, Saudi Arabia, Syria, Turkey, and the United Arab Emirates did not exist before 1914—they became independent between 1920 and 1971. Others, such as Egypt and Iran, were dominated by outside powers until well after World War II. Before 1914, most of the region's states were either controlled by the Turkish-run Ottoman Empire or owed allegiance to the Ottoman sultan. (The sultan was also the caliph or highest religious authority in Islam, in the line of the prophet Muhammad's successors, according to the beliefs of the majority of Muslims known as the Sunni.) It was this imperial Muslim system that was ended by the largely British military victory over the Ottomans in World War I. Few of the leaders who emerged in the wake of this event were happy with the territories they were assigned or the borders, which were often drawn by Europeans. Yet, the system has endured despite many efforts to change it.

The second observation has to do with economics, demography, and natural resources. The Middle Eastern peoples live in a region of often dramatic geographical contrasts: vast parched deserts and high mountains, some with year-round snow; stone-hard volcanic rifts and lush semi-tropical valleys; extremely dry and extremely wet conditions, sometimes separated by only a few miles; large permanent rivers and wadis, riverbeds dry as a bone until winter rains send torrents of flood from the mountains to the sea. In ancient times, a very skilled agriculture made the Middle East the breadbasket of the Roman Empire, and its trade carried luxury fabrics, foods, and spices both East and West.

Most recently, however, the Middle East has become more known for a single commodity—oil, which is unevenly distributed and largely concentrated in the Persian Gulf and Arabian Peninsula (although large pockets are also to be found in Algeria, Libya, and other sites). There are also new, potentially lucrative offshore gas fields in the Eastern Mediterranean.

This uneven distribution of wealth has been compounded by demographics. Birth rates are very high, but the countries with the most oil are often lightly populated. Over the last decade, Middle East populations under the age of 20 have grown enormously. How will these young people be educated? Where will they work? The

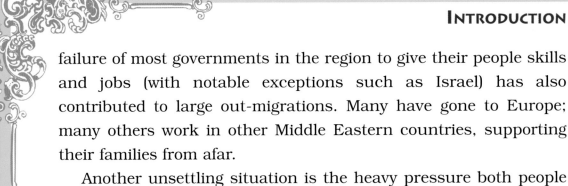

failure of most governments in the region to give their people skills and jobs (with notable exceptions such as Israel) has also contributed to large out-migrations. Many have gone to Europe; many others work in other Middle Eastern countries, supporting their families from afar.

Another unsettling situation is the heavy pressure both people and industry have put on vital resources. Chronic water shortages plague the region. Air quality, public sanitation, and health services in the big cities are also seriously overburdened. There are solutions to these problems, but they require a cooperative approach that is sorely lacking.

A third important observation is the role of religion in the Middle East. Americans, who take separation of church and state for granted, should know that most countries in the region either proclaim their countries to be Muslim or allow a very large role for that religion in public life. Among those with predominantly Muslim populations, Turkey alone describes itself as secular and prohibits avowedly religious parties in the political system. Lebanon was a Christian-dominated state, and Israel continues to be a Jewish state. While both strongly emphasize secular politics, religion plays an enormous role in culture, daily life, and legislation. It is also important to recall that Islamic law (*Sharia*) permits people to practice Judaism and Christianity in Muslim states but only as *Dhimmi*, protected but very second-class citizens.

Fourth, the American student of the modern Middle East will be impressed by the varieties of one-man, centralized rule, very unlike the workings of Western democracies. There are monarchies, some with traditional methods of consultation for tribal elders and even ordinary citizens, in Saudi Arabia and many Gulf States; kings with limited but still important parliaments (such as in Jordan and

Introduction

Morocco); and military and civilian dictatorships, some (such as Syria) even operating on the hereditary principle (Hafez al Assad's son Bashar succeeded him). Turkey is a practicing democracy, although a special role is given to the military that limits what any government can do. Israel operates the freest democracy, albeit constricted by emergency regulations (such as military censorship) due to the Arab-Israeli conflict.

In conclusion, the MODERN MIDDLE EAST NATIONS series will engage imagination and interest simply because it covers an area of such great importance to the United States. Americans may be relative latecomers to the affairs of this region, but our involvement there will endure. We at the Foreign Policy Research Institute hope that these books will kindle a lifelong interest in the fascinating and significant Middle East.

A protester waves the Palestinian flag and flashes the victory sign in Gaza City, 1988. The struggle to obtain a state of their own has been at the heart of the recent history of the Palestinians, a people with ancient ties to Palestine.

Place in the World

*T*heir numbers are relatively small—fewer than 8 million people worldwide—and they have never had an independent state of their own. Yet the Palestinians figure prominently in the strategic concerns of many of the world's most powerful countries, including the United States. Some analysts believe that the plight of the Palestinians is central to the overall prospects for peace and stability in the vital Middle East, and it may be an important factor in the success or failure of America's so-called war on terrorism.

WHO ARE THE PALESTINIANS?

The Palestinians are Arabs who currently live, or whose ancestors lived, in the eastern Mediterranean land called Palestine. Rather than signifying a country with clearly delineated borders, Palestine historically referred to a region, whose limits were somewhat vague and shifted over time.

(The term itself dates only to the second century A.D., by which time the land had already been occupied for millennia.) Today Palestine as a region is generally taken to refer to the territory composed roughly of Israel and the area west of the Jordan River called the West Bank.

The Palestinians say their origins in this land extend all the way back to the Canaanites, a **Semitic** people who occupied parts of Palestine as early as 3000 B.C. That claim, which has political significance, is impossible to prove conclusively. But it is indisputable that Palestinian Arabs have maintained an unbroken presence on the land going back more than a millennium.

Before the 20th century, however, the Palestinians had no sense of a national identity. For 400 years the region was ruled by the Turkish Ottoman Empire, which was centered in Istanbul, and local people identified themselves not as members of a unique Arab group with a specific history and aspirations, but as members of a family, clan, or tribe.

NEIGHBORS AND ENEMIES

The modern history of the Palestinians is inextricably linked to the history of another people with ancient ties to Palestine: the Jews. Around 1200 B.C. a loose-knit collection of Semitic tribes called the Hebrews entered the land of Canaan (the territory between the Mediterranean Sea and the Jordan River) from Egypt. At the center of Hebrew life was a unique religion, Judaism, the world's first **monotheistic** faith. The Hebrews believed that God had established a special covenant, or agreement, with them that, among other things, promised them the land of Canaan.

Over the next two centuries, one of the Hebrew groups, the Israelites, conquered the other peoples of the region and, under King David, set up a powerful kingdom. From their capital in Jerusalem, the Israelites controlled not just Palestine but also parts

Arab leaders (from left: Muammar Qaddafi of Libya, PLO chairman Yasir Arafat, President Gamal Abdel Nasser of Egypt, King Hussein of Jordan) meet in Cairo, Egypt, to discuss an end to the Palestinian-Jordanian civil war, September 27, 1970. The Palestinian national movement, which has spawned much violence with Israel, has also at times bedeviled the Arab world.

of present-day Jordan, Syria, Lebanon, and Iraq. After the death of David's successor, Solomon, the Israelite kingdom was divided into the northern Kingdom of Israel and the southern Kingdom of Judah. While the former was destroyed in the eighth century B.C. by the Assyrians, the latter survived until 586 B.C., when the Babylonians conquered it. At that time, the Jews (the term for the people comes from *Judah*) were removed from their land and taken into bondage in Babylonia.

Six decades later, however, the Persian Empire conquered Babylonia, and the Jews were allowed to return to Palestine. There they enjoyed a fair degree of ***autonomy*** under the rule of various foreign empires until the second century A.D., when the Romans brutally suppressed a Jewish uprising and expelled most of the Jews from their land.

Over the ensuing centuries, the exiled Jews established communities in countries all over the world, even as a smaller Jewish community remained in Palestine. Many Jews hoped to return to their ancestral homeland, and during the 13th and 16th centuries, under the Ottomans, Palestine saw notable waves of Jewish immigration. In the last years of the 19th century and the first decades of the 20th, a movement developed, primarily among European Jews, to establish an independent state for the Jewish people in Palestine.

As Jewish immigrants began settling in the region in larger numbers, particularly after World War I, the Palestinians—who for centuries had lived under rule by a succession of foreign conquerors, including the Byzantines, the crusaders, and the Ottoman Turks—began to see themselves as a distinct national group. And, increasingly, they came to view large-scale Jewish immigration as a threat to their interests. Violence erupted.

Efforts by the international community to create independent homelands in Palestine for both the Jews and the Palestinians led only to war in 1948. In the aftermath of that conflict, the Jewish state, Israel, stood firmly established. The Palestinians, meanwhile, had lost everything. The territory set aside for their homeland was now under the control of Israel, Jordan, and Egypt, and hundreds of thousands of Palestinians were refugees.

Over the next half-century, however, the Palestinians managed to keep alive their sense of identity and their aspirations for a homeland. A campaign of "national liberation," which included **terrorism,** produced no tangible military gains but made it impossible for Israel—or the rest of the world—to ignore the Palestinians. Diplomatic recognition of the dominant Palestinian group, the

Palestine Liberation Organization (PLO), came in the mid-1970s with admission into the Arab League and the granting of observer status at the United Nations.

Originally, the PLO refused to compromise with the Jewish state: it claimed that all Israeli territory legitimately belonged to the Palestinians, and its charter called for the complete destruction of Israel. But an apparent shift in policy occurred in the 1980s and 1990s (though some Israelis continue to be skeptical of Palestinian intentions). The PLO recognized the right of Israel to exist, and, as part of a broad framework for peace called the Oslo accords that was agreed to in 1993, Israel began turning over some territory it occupied to what became known as the Palestinian Authority. A transitional period of limited self-rule was supposed to lead eventually to final-status negotiations over an independent Palestinian state. But a variety of contentious issues remained unresolved. A deadly cycle of Palestinian violence and Israeli retaliation exploded in September 2000, and by early 2003 lasting peace between Israelis and Palestinians seemed only a distant possibility.

The Israeli-Palestinian relationship, which has been poisoned by decades of violence, involves many competing claims. At the heart of the conflict, however, is land.

A Palestinian farmer with an armful of red peppers, Gaza Strip. With its mild winters and hot summers, Gaza produces olives, citrus fruits, and vegetables. Overall, about half the land in the proposed state of Palestine is used for cultivation.

The Land

A s noted earlier, the precise meaning of the term *Palestine*—which dates to A.D. 135, during the Roman era—has changed over time. Roman Palestine was a region that included the territory of modern-day Israel, eastern Jordan, and southern Lebanon, along with the West Bank and Gaza Strip. After World War I, when Great Britain was given a **mandate** to govern Palestine by the United Nations, the territory basically embraced all of modern Israel, Jordan, the West Bank, and Gaza. In 1923 the British split the region into two parts, calling the eastern part Transjordan (today's Jordan) and the western part Palestine (today's Israel, West Bank, and Gaza Strip). It is this Palestine that frames the modern Palestinian-Israeli struggle—or, at least, this was the land involved in the modern dispute.

The rhetoric of hard-liners notwithstanding, the issue of whether Palestinians will one day establish a state embracing all of former British Mandate Palestine is settled: they won't. The State of Israel is firmly established, and all serious proposals for an independent Palestinian homeland center on two parcels of territory: the Gaza Strip and the West Bank. When discussing the Palestinians' land, therefore, it is logical to focus on these two zones.

THE GAZA STRIP

Located along the Mediterranean coast north of Egypt's Sinai Peninsula, the Gaza Strip is a small, rectangular piece of land some 18 miles (29 kilometers) long and 5 miles (8 km) wide. In total area it is only about twice the size of Washington, D.C. Gaza's border with Egypt runs 6.8 miles (11 km); its border with Israel extends 31.7 miles (51 km).

Part of a coastal plain, Gaza features flat or gently rolling terrain. Much of it is covered in sand or sand dunes. However, Gaza

The Geography of the Gaza Strip

Location: Middle East, bordering the Mediterranean Sea, between Egypt and Israel
Area: (slightly more than twice the size of Washington, D.C.)
    total: 139 square miles (360 sq km)
    land: 139 square miles (360 sq km)
    water: 0 square miles
Borders: Egypt, 6.8 miles (11 km); Israel, 31.7 miles (51 km)
Climate: temperate, with mild winters, dry and warm to hot summers
Terrain: flat to rolling, sand- and dune-covered coastal plain
Elevation extremes:
    lowest point: Mediterranean Sea—0 feet
    highest point: Abu 'Awdah (Joz Abu 'Auda)—344 feet (105 meters)
Natural hazards: droughts

Source: Adapted from CIA World Factbook, 2002.

A view of Jenin, an important Palestinian town located in the hills of the northern West Bank.

enjoys a temperate climate, with mild winters and warm to hot summers, and some of the land is cultivated. Citrus fruit, olives, and vegetables are among its most important crops.

With its teeming refugee camps and urban areas, the Gaza Strip's overall population density exceeds 8,000 people per square mile (more than 3,000 people per square kilometer). This makes it one of the world's most crowded places.

THE WEST BANK

About the size of Delaware in total area, the West Bank is 16 times larger than the Gaza Strip, from which it is separated by more than 20 miles (32 km) at the closest point. Its eastern border with Jordan is 60 miles (97 km) long and is formed by the Jordan River and the Dead Sea. On the north, east, and south, the West Bank is surrounded by Israel, a border of 191 miles (307 km).

Unlike the relatively flat Gaza Strip, the West Bank is composed largely of rugged hills. Over the centuries, the Palestinians tended to make their homes in the more easily defended hill country, which not only offered them protection from raiding **Bedouin** nomads but also kept them more independent from the various empires that controlled the region. Historically, major Palestinian settlements developed in four hill regions: Al Jaleel (Galilee), Jabal Nablus, Jabal al-Quds (Jerusalem), and Jabal al-Khalil (Hebron). Of these, Galilee (to the north) is outside any proposed Palestinian homeland, and Jerusalem is bitterly disputed territory.

Historically, most Palestinians were farmers and livestock herders who lived in small villages that surrounded larger towns. They cultivated olive and almond trees near their homes or grew cotton, wheat, corn, barley, and sesame on the nearby plains. Over time, the hill communities developed into major cities. Today these cities include Ramallah, Bethlehem, and Jenin.

GEOGRAPHICAL ZONES

In addition to the coastal region of the Gaza Strip, the proposed Palestinian homeland may be divided into four geographical zones in the West Bank: the Jordan River valley, the eastern slopes region, the central highlands region, and the semi-coastal region. There are very few natural resources in any of these zones, except for arable land. About half the land in the West Bank and Gaza is used for cultivation. Of this land, 60 percent is irrigated and is used to grow mostly citrus fruits and grains. Much of the portion that isn't irrigated is used to grow olives, grapes, and almonds.

The Jordan River valley, at the eastern end of the West Bank, has been the home of farmers for more than 10,000 years. Although the average yearly rainfall is only 12 inches (30.5 cm), the Jordan River valley has excellent climatic conditions for cultivating crops, with hot summers and short, mild winters. Humidity is good for certain crops, and the heat in this region is humid because there is a hothouse effect, caused by the steep cliff face that borders the region on both the east and west. Today, Palestinian farmers of this region grow vegetables and semitropical fruits like citrus fruits and bananas.

West of the Jordan River valley is the eastern slopes region, an area of hills and valleys running from the area east of the city of Jenin in the north to the eastern Hebron district in the south. The elevation here ranges from 2,400 feet (732 meters) above sea level to 450 feet (137 meters) below sea level. The semiarid climate has a low annual rainfall, making it less desirable for cultivation. Although this region is mostly used for grazing sheep and goats, some native plants such as pistachio trees and thyme are cultivated here.

The central highlands region forms the spine of historical Palestine, and it is the largest, most densely populated region in the West Bank today. Its ancient cities were settled by one of the earliest known tribes of the region, the Canaanites, as early as 5,000 years ago. It is a mountainous region that extends from Jenin to Hebron, with elevations exceeding 3,000 feet (915 meters). For

The Geography of the West Bank

Location: Middle East, west of Jordan
Area: (slightly smaller than Delaware)
  total: 2,263 square miles (5,860 sq km)
  land: 2,176 square miles (5,640 sq km)
  water: 85 square miles (220 sq km)
Borders: Israel, 191 miles (307 km); Jordan, 60 miles (97 km)
Climate: temperate; temperature and precipitation vary with altitude; warm to hot summers, cool to mild winters
Terrain: mostly rugged dissected upland; some vegetation in west, but barren in east
Elevation extremes:
  lowest point: Dead Sea—1,339 feet (408 meters) below sea level
  highest point: Tall Asur—3,353 feet (1,022 meters)
Natural hazards: droughts

Source: Adapted from CIA World Factbook, 2002.

thousands of years, this region has been highly cultivated because it receives an adequate annual rainfall for a variety of crops, and it has good soil for farming. The main crops are olives and grapes, which are grown in terraced vineyards. There are also orchards for almond and fruit trees, and fields of grain and **legumes** are common. To a lesser extent, vegetables are also grown in the West Bank's central highlands.

The semi-coastal region is the smallest portion of the West Bank, covering only the northwest corner from Jenin to Tulkarem. This is part of the Mediterranean coastal region that stretches from the coast of Israel eastward to the slopes of the highlands. Compared with the highland region, this area is relatively flat and has little rainfall. Farmers rely on irrigation to cultivate their citrus orchards and vegetable farms. Some legumes and grains are also cultivated here.

Olives have probably been cultivated in the hill country of historic Palestine for nearly 5,000 years. Olive trees can range from 10 to 40 feet (3 to 12 meters) in height and can grow to be hundreds of years old because the wood of the olive tree resists decay so well. Olive oil is a major export crop in this region. Once, olive oil was an essential ingredient for making soap. Today, most olive oil is used in cooking and processing food.

ENVIRONMENTAL ISSUES

The West Bank and Gaza Strip face many environmental problems. In the Gaza Strip, these problems include desertification (the encroachment of desert sands), salinization of freshwater aquifers through the seeping into the water table of Mediterranean saltwater, and soil depletion from years of intensive farming. In the West Bank, the most important environmental issues include sewage treatment problems and limits to the freshwater supply.

Limited water has been a reality in this dry region for thousands of years, but in modern times, with increased population, the situation has become more acute. And water, like so much else in Palestinian-Israeli relations, has been a source of bitterness and conflict. The West Bank has two major **aquifers**. Not only do these aquifers supply water for the Palestinians, but they also provide about 40 percent of Israel's total water needs. The Palestinians charge that Israel, which since 1967 has controlled the West Bank aquifers, takes more than its fair share and that, by design or by accident, its water policies have had a devastating impact on Palestinian farmers. After 1967 Israel drilled deep wells, which had the effect of siphoning off water from old Palestinian wells. At the same time, Israel made it illegal for the Palestinians to drill their own newer, deeper wells. Israeli restrictions on water use forced many Palestinian farmers to stop cultivating formerly irrigated land—which some Palestinians believed was a way for Israel ultimately to get control of their land.

In spite of the density of the population and the environmental problems in the West Bank and Gaza, there are pockets of wilderness where wildlife still roams. Mammals include the ibex, mountain gazelle, jackal, fox, wildcat, hedgehog, and wild hare. The mountain gazelle, praised in Arabic poetry for its speed and beauty, lives in the mountains and plains in the south and east of the West Bank. The Palestine jungle cat, a small, short-tailed wildcat, roams the reed beds of the Jordan River. Another rare wildcat, the Sinai leopard, lives in the Judean desert region near the Dead Sea in the southern portion of the West Bank. Palestinian scientists, working with other scientists in the Arab world, have been attempting to identify, count, and protect the remaining wildlife that coexists with the Palestinian people.

Over the course of thousands of years, Palestine has felt the influence of many powerful peoples and empires. Hisham's Palace, pictured here, was built near Jericho as a winter residence for the caliphs of the Damascus-based Arab Omayyad dynasty. Though much of the complex was destroyed by an earthquake in 747, the surviving floor mosaics hint at the splendor of early Islamic art and architecture.

History

Historic Palestine is part of a region called the Fertile Crescent, where the earliest human civilizations are thought to have begun. Its eastern border, along the Jordan River valley, was settled around 8000 B.C. This land was not only the site of the earliest agricultural communities but also the home to some of the first cities. Jericho, now in the area known as the West Bank, may be the world's oldest walled city.

Around 2000 B.C., these early urban cultures moved or died out, and Semitic-speaking nomads moved into the area. Although they had similar cultures, these tribes—the Amorites, Canaanites, Hebrews, Ammonites, Moabites, Edomites, and Arameans—were often at war with one another. Eventually, the Israelites conquered their neighbors and established an enduring Jewish culture whose spiritual and political center was in Jerusalem.

But over the next two millennia, a succession of powerful invaders conquered all or parts of Palestine. The inhabitants of the region, the descendants of the earlier tribal peoples, resisted or adapted to their conquerors.

Around 722 B.C. the Assyrians conquered northern Palestine. Nearly 100 years later the Babylonians defeated the Assyrians and destroyed the city of Jerusalem. The mighty Persian Empire soon followed. In 334 B.C. the Greek armies of Alexander the Great swept through Palestine. Alexander, a Macedonian, introduced the ideals and culture of Greece to the area.

In the first century B.C., another rising Mediterranean power, Rome, took control of Palestine. It was during the Roman era that Christianity emerged in Palestine. Christianity's central figure, a Jew named Jesus of Nazareth, was, his followers came to believe, the Son of God, sent to redeem sinful humanity. Around A.D. 30, Jesus was executed, buried, and, his followers claimed, rose from the dead in Jerusalem, making that city holy ground for Christians as well as Jews.

In 135, after bitter fighting, Rome suppressed a Jewish revolt, destroyed Jerusalem (including the Jews' Holy Temple), renamed the area Palestine (after the Jews' traditional enemies, the Philistines), and expelled many Jews from the region. Initially, the **pagan** Romans also persecuted members of the new Christian faith, but in the fourth century Christianity became the official religion of the Roman Empire. In Palestine, Christianity became the dominant religion in towns and cities, but most rural peoples continued to practice traditional cult religions.

THE COMING OF ISLAM

The religion that has had the most profound and lasting influence on Palestinian culture, however, originated on the Arabian Peninsula during the seventh century. Around the year 610,

Muhammad, a merchant living in Mecca (in modern-day Saudi Arabia), received the first in a series of revelations from Allah (God). Shortly thereafter he began to preach Allah's message, the essence of which is that there is only one God and that people must submit to God's will (the word *Islam* means "submission"). The Arabs of the time worshiped many gods, and initially Muhammad's message was met with hostility. He and his followers, called Muslims, were forced from Mecca and settled in the town of Medina in 622. After a period of warfare, however, the Muslims triumphed, bringing Mecca and the entire Arabian Peninsula under the influence of Islam.

After Muhammad's death in 632, Arab Muslim armies swept forth from the peninsula, conquering and converting peoples in North Africa and the Mediterranean region to their new faith.

Around A.D. 610 Muhammad, an Arab living in Mecca, was visited in a cave by an angel who commanded him to proclaim the word of Allah (God). That event, depicted in this colored engraving, led to the foundation of Islam. After the Prophet's death in 632, his followers spread the new religion. Palestine was one of the first regions outside the Arabian Peninsula to be conquered.

Palestine was one of the first places conquered by the Islamic armies, which occupied Jerusalem by A.D. 638. That city held special significance for Muslims as well as Jews and Christians. It was from Jerusalem, Muslims believe, that Muhammad ascended to heaven after a nighttime journey on a flying stallion. Thus, in 691, a mosque, or Muslim place of worship, was constructed over the ground from which Muhammad is said to have departed. (That mosque, the Dome of the Rock, is part of the Al-Aqsa complex, which is located on the area Jews call the Temple Mount and

Built in 691 over the place where Muhammad is said to have ascended to heaven, the magnificent Dome of the Rock is one of Jerusalem's most recognizable landmarks. The mosque sits in an area both Muslims and Jews consider sacred ground—a fact that has caused considerable friction between Palestinians and Israelis.

consider their faith's holiest site. Needless to say, that has caused much friction between Palestinian Muslims and Israeli Jews.)

After the Arab conquest, most of Palestine's inhabitants converted to the new faith, though small communities of Jews and Christians remained. Under Islamic rule, these non-Muslim communities paid a poll tax and faced certain legal restrictions, but they often thrived commercially.

Although Islamic armies conquered huge swaths of North Africa, the Middle East, and even Spain in a remarkably short time, the Islamic world did not remain united for long. After Muhammad's death, there had been disagreement over who should be caliph, the Prophet's successor as the head of the Islamic faith. The caliph had a religious role, in guarding the traditions of the prophet Muhammad and enforcing Islamic holy law, or **Sharia**. But he also had a political role, as the supreme governor of Islamic lands.

As the Islamic empire expanded, different clans established rival caliphates, as their governments were called. The first Islamic caliphate, which was established in Damascus, was called the Omayyad Caliphate; it was named for the powerful clan that eventually conquered and ruled all of the Arabian Peninsula, northern Africa, and southern Europe.

The Abbasids, a rival clan, overthrew the Omayyads in 750, moving the caliphate to Baghdad in what is now Iraq. In Palestine, this change caused an increase in raiding from nomadic Bedouins, and many people retreated from their towns and villages to the safety of the mountainous regions in central Palestine. The area was taken over by the Fatimids of Egypt in the 9th century, then by the Seljuk Turks in the 11th century. Christian invaders from Europe were the next conquerors, though their control was brief. During the First Crusade, European Christians captured Jerusalem in 1099. A century later, Saladin, the Islamic ruler of Egypt, defeated the Crusaders and retook Jerusalem in 1187.

Fighting between Christians and Muslims continued in Palestine for another 100 years.

PALESTINE UNDER THE OTTOMAN EMPIRE

This period of continually shifting imperial control in Palestine came to an end in the mid-1500s with the arrival of the Ottoman Empire. The Ottomans—Muslims, but Turks rather than Arabs—maintained their capital in far-off Istanbul, where their supreme ruler, the sultan, lived. To administer their vast empire the Ottomans divided their holdings into *vilayets* (provinces) that were ruled by *pashas* (governors). Ultimately, the pashas were accountable to the sultan.

Palestine was part of the *vilayet* of Beirut. At this time, it was a region of rich farmland and villages, with no major city except Jerusalem, which was an important pilgrimage site for Muslims. As in the rest of the Ottoman Empire, Muslims in Palestine were bound by the laws of *Sharia.* Other religious communities paid a special tax but were permitted significant autonomy in religious matters.

Arabs loyal to the Ottoman sultan ruled Palestine for nearly 400 years. The empire's presence was felt mostly through the heavy taxes its subjects were forced to pay. As much as two-thirds of Palestine's income from agriculture went to the payment of taxes. Occasional tax rebellions were harshly put down. But the empire did little to change or modernize this region.

By the 19th century, most of Palestine's population was concentrated in protected hill country of what was called Judea, Samaria, and upper Galilee. The coastal regions were exposed to Bedouin raiders, and the countryside between the towns belonged to Bedouins. Because of the tax system, wealthy families had gained control of much of the land, with some peasants continuing to work land they no longer owned. Many other landless peasants moved into the cities and coastal towns.

In 1831 Muhammad Ali, the pasha of Egypt, conquered Palestine and welcomed Westerners as foreign investors. He attempted to modernize the region and to control Bedouin raiding. In 1838 Ali Pasha declared independence from the Ottomans, but he soon had to relinquish Palestine after being defeated by the armies of the Ottoman sultan and the British navy.

However, Ali Pasha had opened Palestine to the modern world, and to Europe in particular. In 1838 Great Britain opened a consulate (an office established primarily to represent its citizens' commercial interests) in Jerusalem. Other European countries soon established a presence there as well, stating the need to protect the interests of Christians in Palestine. Britain took up the Jewish cause, claiming an obligation to protect Jews in the region. By the end of the 19th century, European commercial power and influence in Palestine had begun to cause tension with the local Arab population.

ZIONISM AND THE PALESTINIANS

The end of the 19th century also saw the beginnings, in Europe, of a movement that would eventually change the history of Palestine: *Zionism*. After being removed from Palestine by the Romans in the second century A.D., Jews had eventually settled in many countries around the world. But because of their religious and cultural traditions, they frequently maintained distinct and easily identified communities within the societies in which they lived, and they were often the targets of discrimination, harassment, and even pogroms (organized massacres). Some Jews, primarily from Europe, started to consider the possibility of establishing their own homeland, where they would be free from such persecution. And the most logical place seemed to be Palestine, a land to which they had deep and ancient ties. As Jews traditionally called this land Zion, the movement to reestablish a Jewish homeland there was known as Zionism and its advocates as Zionists.

As early as the 1870s, Jews from Europe bought land in Palestine, hoping to set up a Jewish community there as a refuge. But the Zionist movement only began to gather momentum as a result of the efforts of a Hungarian-born journalist named Theodor Herzl. In 1897 Herzl organized the Zionist World Congress in Basel, Switzerland. From that meeting emerged the Zionist Organization, dedicated to building a Jewish state in Palestine. Herzl served as the group's president until his death in 1904.

As Zionism gradually captured the imagination of European Jews, Jewish settlers began arriving in large numbers in Palestine. The persecution of Jews in Russia brought more than 30,000 educated, hardworking Jews to the region by 1914. By that time Jews made up 12 percent of the population of the region. Political tension and open conflict grew between organized, nationalistic Jewish settlers and native Arabs, many of whom resented the newcomers' presence on land they thought of as theirs. As the Jewish population increased, glimmers of Arab Palestinian nationalism arose. For the first time Palestinians began using the word *Filastin* to refer to their country, as a way of distinguishing themselves from, and uniting against, outsiders.

WORLD WAR I AND THE BRITISH MANDATE

Before the friction between the Zionists and Arab nationalists erupted into a full-scale conflict, World War I broke out, in August 1914. The war pitted Great Britain, France, Russia, and later the United States against Germany, Austria-Hungary, and the Ottoman Empire, which still claimed political control of Palestine. In order to undermine the Ottomans, British authorities incited a rebellion among Arabs in the Middle East. At the center of that uprising was the Hashemite family, traditional guardians of Muslim

The Hungarian-born Jewish writer Theodor Herzl is considered the father of Zionism, the movement to establish a homeland for Jews in Palestine.

holy sites in Mecca. In return for their support, the British promised the Hashemites that they would support the creation of an Arab state after the war. Meanwhile, in 1917, the British issued the Balfour Declaration, which read, "His Majesty's Government view with favour the establishment in Palestine of a national home for the Jewish people, and will use their best endeavours to facilitate the achievement of this object, it being clearly understood that nothing shall be done which may prejudice the civil and religious rights of existing non-Jewish communities in Palestine, or the rights and political status enjoyed by Jews in any other country."

Britain's promises to the Arabs and the Zionists were not necessarily incompatible—the boundaries of the future Arab state were vague, and the Balfour Declaration did not advocate a Jewish state that encompassed all of Palestine. Nevertheless, many people on both sides would come to question the intentions of the British. Indeed, Great Britain had its own interests in the region apart from fulfilling its wartime promises. Specifically, British leaders saw control of Palestine as key to (1) protecting their country's route, via the Suez Canal, to the important British colony of India; (2) having access to a cheap source of oil in what is now Iraq; and (3) expanding British economic interests in the region.

And by the end of World War I in 1918, Britain was in actual control of Palestine, having won the region militarily from Ottoman forces the previous year. By the terms of the peace treaty that officially ended the war, the Middle East possessions of the defeated Ottoman Empire were divided principally between Britain and France (which was also in keeping with the secret Sykes-Picot agreement the two countries had concluded during the war). Technically, British and French authority derived from the mandates granted them by the newly formed **League of Nations**. In return for the right to administer the territories, the European countries were supposed to develop the local economy and political organization. In the case of Palestine, Britain was also supposed to facilitate the creation of a Jewish homeland, an obligation that was written into the Mandate terms. The Mandate included the establishment of the Jewish Agency, which had the effect of creating a Jewish government in Palestine. Because Palestine was an underdeveloped country, British authorities and many Zionists believed that Jewish-based development would enrich the economy, sustain a much larger population, and make Jewish colonization acceptable to the Arab population.

No equivalent agency was set up for the Arab population. However, during this time, the political climate in Palestine was charged with ideas of nationhood, self-determination, and reform. This was the beginning of the modern idea of a Palestinian identity. At this time, the population of war-damaged Palestine was

573,000 Arabs (of whom 61,000 were Christian and the rest Muslim) and 66,000 Jews. One-quarter of the region's population had died during the war. Two-thirds of the Palestinian population consisted of impoverished peasants. As the British reorganized Palestine during the early years of the Mandate, they gave money, jobs, and power to influential Muslims and Christians. Rather than build a sense of national unity, these wealthy Palestinians worked to increase their own power. In contrast, the Zionists built on the structure of the Jewish Agency to create a politically organized Jewish community.

Neither the powerful Arabs nor the British did much to improve

British Mandate soldiers try to contain a riot at Jerusalem's Jaffa Gate. Increased Jewish immigration and economic difficulties among resident Arabs were among the factors that fueled rising violence between Palestinians and Zionists during the 1920s and 1930s.

the daily life of most Arab Palestinians, and during the 1920s a big gap developed between the Arab and Jewish standard of living. Many factors contributed to this situation. One was labor inequality: Arab capitalists employed the overwhelming majority of Arab workers, and they offered lower wages than those paid by Jewish employers to Jewish workers. Per capita income was three times higher for Jews than for Arabs. Also, British Mandate authorities gave more support to Jewish health and educational services than to Arab social services. By the 1930s, more than 80 percent of Arab peasants were illiterate, a situation that did not particularly concern the Arab wealthy class. At the same time, Arab absentee landowners sold their land to Jewish settlers at an ever-increasing rate, forcing thousands of Palestinian peasants to the cities. Frustration and poverty convinced many of them that it would be impossible to share Palestine with the Jews.

The first major clash between Arabs and Jews under British military rule took place in 1920, during a Muslim festival near Jerusalem. The festival procession turned into bloody rioting, with five Jews and four Arabs killed. This incident spurred the Zionists to acquire weapons and train militarily. More rioting took place in Jaffa in 1921, with 47 Jews and 48 Arabs killed. In 1929 further riots in Jerusalem claimed the lives of 133 Jews and 116 Arabs. After each outbreak of violence, the British tried to appease Arab Palestinians by limiting Jewish immigration. This angered the Zionists, who felt that the British were reneging on their earlier promises set forth in the Balfour Declaration.

But Jewish immigration to Palestine surged in the mid-1930s, following the rise of the Nazis in Germany. Many Jews moved to urban centers and prospered because they had money and technical skills. They purchased land carefully, looking for high-quality property that was near other Jewish settlements. By 1936 a quarter million Jews had immigrated to Palestine.

THE ARAB REVOLT AND BRITAIN'S WITHDRAWAL

That same year, Palestinian Arabs took up arms against both the Zionists and British in what came to be called the Great Arab Revolt. The root causes were Arab frustration with Britain's policies, which had done nothing to advance the Palestinians toward self-rule; the terrible economic situation of peasants and workers; and anxiety about the possibility of a Jewish majority if large-scale immigration continued. The British military, the Zionist **paramilitary** force known as the Haganah, and British-trained Jewish civilian militias used tough measures to put down the rebellion, which ended as World War II began in 1939.

For the Palestinians, the revolt was a failure. In the three years of fighting, more than 5,000 Arabs had died in raids and clashes. Not only was the Palestinian military effort highly disorganized, but the Palestinians lacked a unifying political **ideology** for creating an independent state. By contrast, the Zionists had such an ideology, and the Haganah, which had been founded in 1920, was by this time a well-commanded and effective military organization. In addition, the British authorities helped to train and equip Zionist militias, and the British also confiscated quantities of Arab arms and ammunition and exiled Arab Palestinian leaders. Making matters worse, the Palestinian economy collapsed with the Great Depression, and by 1939, most Palestinians were even poorer than before.

The Arab Revolt spurred Britain to reevaluate the Palestine Mandate. As early as 1937, the Peel Commission, a British group appointed to study the Zionist-Palestinian problem, issued a report recommending the **partition** of Palestine into a Jewish and a Palestinian Arab state, with the British maintaining control of a corridor from Jaffa to Jerusalem. Ultimately the Palestinians rejected the Peel Commission plans. In 1939 another committee of British diplomats recommended that Britain's goal be to help set up self-government by the resident populations of Palestine, including the establishment of a Palestinian state. At the same time, Britain tried to limit Jewish immigration, despite the growing persecution of Jews in Europe by Nazi Germany. These policies angered many Zionists, whose leadership worked secretly to circumvent the immigration restrictions.

World War II (1939–45) dramatically altered the situation in Palestine. The Holocaust, Nazi Germany's attempt to exterminate all of Europe's Jews, claimed the lives of as many as 6 million. As the world became aware of the scope of the horror, sympathy ran high for the plight of European Jews—some 250,000 of whom languished in displaced-person camps, waiting for a chance to emigrate, after

British soldiers search for survivors amid the ruins of Jerusalem's King David Hotel, destroyed in July 1946 in a bombing carried out by the Zionist paramilitary group Irgun. After World War II the British Mandate administration faced increased opposition from both Jews and Palestinians, a major factor in Britain's decision to withdraw from Palestine.

the war's end. Despite worldwide pressure to increase Jewish immigration quotas to Palestine, the British resisted. The British were still trying to satisfy Arabs and Zionists, but they succeeded in satisfying neither.

Zionist paramilitary groups began attacking infrastructure (such as rail lines), British personnel, and even Arab villages. In July 1946 the Zionist group Irgun carried out perhaps the most notorious of these attacks: the bombing of the King David Hotel in Jerusalem, where the British maintained a command center; the blast killed more than 90 British, Arabs, and Jews. In the wake of the campaign of violence, Britain decreased its support for the Zionists, who began to look instead toward the United States for support.

As the Zionists became more militant, so too did the Palestinian Arabs. But a lack of organization and unity of ideals weakened the Palestinian cause.

Similarly, Arabs outside of Palestine were less than united. In 1946 the League of Arab States—an organization designed to promote the common interests of Arabs—was formed. But while the Arab League's founding members—Syria, Egypt, Lebanon, Transjordan, and Iraq—publicly voiced support for the Palestinian cause, they were often more interested in advancing their own goals than in helping the Arab people of Palestine.

By 1947 the Palestine Mandate had become too difficult and expensive for Britain to oversee. Growing unrest and violence required the presence of 100,000 British troops. And with the independence of India, Palestine's strategic value to Britain declined enormously. The British asked the United Nations to intervene in finding a solution to the Palestine situation.

THE U.N. PARTITION PLAN

The U.N. Special Committee on Palestine (UNSCOP) recommended the formation of separate Arab and Jewish states, with

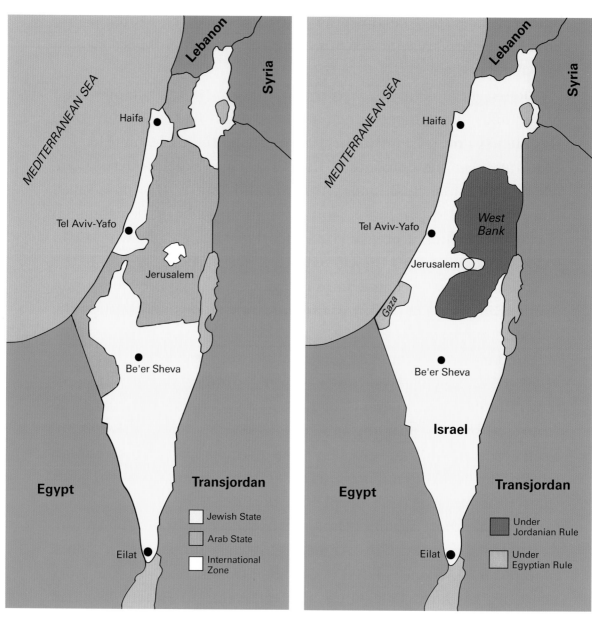

Left: The United Nations partition plan approved in late 1947 allocated half of Palestine for a Jewish state and half for a Palestinian state, with Jerusalem as an international zone. Right: The 1948–49 Arab-Israeli war left the Palestinians with no land at all. At the conclusion of the fighting, Egypt occupied the Gaza Strip, along the Mediterranean coast; Transjordan controlled the area west of the Jordan River; and Israel had taken the rest of the territory set aside for the Palestinian state.

international status for Jerusalem, and economic cooperation between all parties. It was unclear who would enforce the U.N. partition plan after Britain pulled out the following May, but on November 29, 1947, the United Nations General Assembly adopted the plan.

Though not entirely happy with the partition plan, the Zionists said they would accept it. The Arabs, on the other hand, were furious. Representatives of the Arab countries walked out of the General Assembly in protest, and the Arab League vowed to prevent any partition from taking effect.

The terms of the partition, Palestinians claimed, unfairly favored the Zionists. At the time, the total population of the Palestine Mandate was 1.9 million, with 600,000 Jews and 1.3 million Arabs. Eighty-five percent of the Jewish population was centered in three urban areas: Tel Aviv, Jerusalem, and Haifa. Under the U.N. plan, the Jews, who represented 30 percent of the population and owned about 6 percent of the territory, would receive half of Palestine (though, it must be emphasized, much of the land set aside for the Jewish state was in the Negev Desert). Because huge sections of Arab-inhabited land would be transferred to Zionist control, more than a half million Arabs would live in the Jewish state. The Arab state, on the other hand, would include several thousand Jews.

"Al-Nakba"

To this day, the events of 1948 remain the subject of bitter dispute between Palestinians and Israelis. Each side offers a vastly different interpretation of how, and why, what Palestinians call *al-Nakba* ("the disaster") came to pass.

What is certain is that neither the Palestinian Arabs nor the Zionists waited until mid-May—when the partition plan was scheduled to be implemented—to begin fighting. Almost immediately after the November 29, 1947, General Assembly vote, Jewish-Arab violence exploded. While some of the early bloodshed represented spontaneous acts of violence and retaliation, the fighting evolved into a more organized struggle, with Haganah units and smaller Zionist paramilitary groups battling Palestinians in strategic villages and in cities such as Haifa and Acre. By May 1948, the more organized Zionist forces had gotten the upper hand on the Palestinians, who had only a very small trained armed force, no centralized command, and limited arms and ammunition. Some 300,000 Palestinians had abandoned their homes, leaving whole towns and villages empty.

On May 14, 1948, the British officially pulled out of Palestine, and Zionist leaders proclaimed the independence of the State of Israel. As promised, the armies of Arab League members Egypt, Syria, Transjordan, Lebanon, and Iraq moved to crush the new Jewish state, and the fighting in Palestine entered a wider, bloodier phase.

The Arabs won some early victories, but to the surprise of almost everyone, Israeli forces not only held in the face of the Arab onslaught, but actually pushed the Arabs back. By the time the fighting had ended in January 1949, Israel controlled some three-quarters of Palestine, rather than the half allotted it in the partition plan. That did not mean, however, that one-quarter of Palestine remained for a Palestinian homeland. For despite their Pan-Arab rhetoric and expressions of solidarity with the Palestinians, the Arab countries largely pursued their own selfish interests. "What was supposed to be a holy war against the Jews," historian Avi Shlaim has written, "quickly turned into a general land grab." Of the territory set aside for the Palestinians by the U.N. and not conquered by Israel, the rest was taken by two Arab countries: Egypt claimed the Gaza Strip, along the Mediterranean coast, and Transjordan seized the territory west of the Jordan River, including East Jerusalem (Israel held the western part of the city).

The Arab refusal to accept partition had cost Palestinians dearly. Not only did they have no homeland of their own, but about 13,000 Palestinians had been killed. Moreover, 370 Palestinian towns and villages had been depopulated or destroyed, and of a prewar population of some 1.4 million, as many as 750,000 Palestinians were refugees.

To this day, the question of what caused this stream of refugees still evokes vitriolic finger-pointing among Palestinians and Israelis. For years, most Israelis maintained that Arab leaders told Palestinians to temporarily leave their homes in order to make room

Palestinians burn the Israeli flag at a refugee camp in Syria, 2002. The 1948–49 Arab-Israeli war produced the first flood of Palestinian refugees, many of whom ended up in squalid camps in Transjordan, Lebanon, and Syria. Fifty years later, the families of some of the original refugees were still living in these camps.

for the Arab armies to attack the Jews. But research within the last two decades has discredited this explanation, except in a few isolated cases. Now the conventional view among Israeli scholars is that the stream of refugees was an unanticipated and unintended consequence of the war—that the Palestinians, naturally enough, fled their homes out of fear when the fighting approached or arrived. Thus, if anyone is to blame for the refugee problem, most Israelis believe, it is the Palestinians and the Arab countries, because they refused to accept partition and thus unleashed the violence.

Most Palestinians, on the other hand, blame Israel largely or entirely for the refugee problem. They assert that the flood of refugees—before and after May 1948—was neither unanticipated nor unintended. Rather, they claim, emptying strategic areas of their Palestinian inhabitants was a key component of the Zionist military plan. They say the Israelis accomplished this by killing, terrorizing, and at times forcibly expelling Palestinians.

Some support for this viewpoint is found among a controversial group of Jewish scholars known as the "new historians." In his landmark 1987 book, *The Birth of the Palestinian Refugee Problem, 1947–1949*, Benny Morris, the dean of the new historians, attempted to identify the reasons for the emptying of 369 Palestinian towns and villages. Morris concluded that in 11 percent, or 41, of the towns and villages, the Palestinians were forcibly expelled; he found just 6 instances when the residents left their homes at the urging of local Arab authorities. In the vast majority of localities, the Palestinian residents either fled during military actions by Israeli forces (228), or because of panic over fighting in neighboring villages or rumors of Israeli atrocities (90). In 45 cases Morris could not establish the reason the Palestinians left. (The total adds up to more than 369 because multiple causes were assigned for the emptying of some areas.) Morris concluded that, while Israeli leaders weren't unhappy about the exodus of Palestinians, the refugee problem "was born of war, not by design, Jewish or Arab."

Other new historians challenged that conclusion. Ilan Pappe, author of *The Making of the Arab-Israeli Conflict, 1947–1951*, maintained that the Zionist defense strategy known as Plan Dalet, which was created in early 1948, "can be regarded as a master plan for expulsion." It included provisions for

> Destruction of villages (setting fire to, blowing up, and planting mines in the debris), especially those population centers which are difficult to control continuously.

> Mounting search and control operations according to the following guidelines: encirclement of the village and conducting a search inside it. In the event of resistance, the armed force must be destroyed and the population must be expelled outside the borders of the state.

In the opinion of some critics, Benny Morris's distinction between Palestinians who left voluntarily and those who were forcibly expelled is somewhat arbitrary—and often meaningless. When Palestinians fled their homes, some of these critics say, Israelis blocked them from returning—even when the Palestinians were waiting right outside their town or village for fighting there to cease. And with the Palestinians gone, villages were frequently razed or the homes and farmland given to Jewish settlers under an Israeli law that legalized the confiscation of "abandoned properties."

Whether the flood of refugees was the unintended consequence of war or part of an Israeli strategy, the displaced Palestinians—many of whom settled in squalid refugee camps in Arab countries such as Transjordan, Syria, and Lebanon—believed that the world ignored their plight in the decades after *al-Nakba*. Perhaps, the Palestinian historian Rashid Khalidi has written, this is because "the Palestinians were the victims of victims, defeated and dispossessed by the survivors of the modern era's greatest human atrocity, the Holocaust." Not surprisingly, the remarkable story of Israel's founding captured the world's imagination: a people stateless for 2,000 years managed to keep alive their culture and religion, and, on the heels of genocidal persecution and a war to thwart their aspirations, they succeeded in establishing a state located in their ancestral homeland. In this story, Khalidi says, the Palestinians became "an annoying complication, to be written out of the history"—or, even worse, "the villains of the piece, the latest incarnation of a sequence of tormentors who have persecuted the Jewish people."

A PEOPLE WITHOUT A VOICE: 1949–1967

In the years after the first Arab-Israeli war, none of the governments of the defeated Arab countries signed a peace agreement with Israel. Instead, they kept up a steady stream of anti-Israel rhetoric, promising one day to crush the Jewish state. For the approximately 750,000 Palestinian refugees, such talk held out the hope that they would eventually be able to return to their homes and their land. In reality, the prospect of an Arab military defeat of Israel grew more remote with the passage of time. For one thing, large-scale immigration of Jews dramatically increased Israel's population, giving it a bigger pool of potential soldiers. For another, the Arab governments continued to lack a united front as they pursued their own agendas.

Perhaps as many as 200,000 Palestinian Arabs, mostly poor workers and farmers, had remained in Israel after the 1948–49 war. Israel granted these people citizenship rights, and today Arab Israelis constitute nearly 20 percent of the country's population.

Of the Arab states, however, only Jordan (the country's name was officially changed from Transjordan in 1949) offered Palestinians full citizenship. But friction between the Palestinians and the Jordanian government and people was widespread. In addition to the refugees who had fled into Jordan from the territory that became Israel, about 500,000 Palestinians were living in their longtime homes in the Jordanian-occupied West Bank, and these people tended to be better-educated, more urban, and more prosperous than the rest of Jordan's population, much of which was made up of traditionally nomadic Bedouins. In 1950 Jordan annexed the West Bank, extinguishing for the foreseeable future hopes for Palestinian self-government there. The following year a Palestinian extremist assassinated King Abdullah, the Jordanian monarch.

During the 1950s and early 1960s, much of the world continued to see the Palestinian question as a refugee problem, not a national issue. But some Palestinians began organizing themselves with the goal of "liberating" Palestine from Israeli control. And for the heads of various Arab countries, public support of the Palestinian cause became a way to demonstrate their leadership credentials within the Arab world—even if they actually did little in concrete terms to help the Palestinian people.

In 1964 the Palestine Liberation Organization (PLO) was established, principally under Egyptian sponsorship, to coordinate the activities of Palestinian nationalist groups. Soon Syria, unwilling to cede to Egypt leadership of the Palestinian cause, began backing its own Palestinian nationalist group: al-Fatah (the Victory Party). The previously obscure al-Fatah, which had been founded in 1959 by an Egyptian-born Palestinian named Yasir Arafat, began launching guerrilla raids and terrorist attacks inside Israel, upstaging the less active PLO. But, as the Syrians quickly discovered, Arafat refused to take orders from his sponsors, insisting that the Palestinians must control their own destiny. Hafez al-Assad, Syria's defense minister (and later president), ordered Arafat's arrest and conviction for murder in 1966, but under pressure from Palestinian supporters, Arafat was quietly released.

THE SIX-DAY WAR AND ITS AFTERMATH

By 1967 Israel had been in existence for nearly two decades as an independent state, but the Arab countries still refused to recognize it, declaring that they were in a "state of war" with Israel. Tensions escalated in May with a series of bellicose actions and shrill rhetoric initiated by Egypt. As the Arab countries massed their armies near Israel's borders for an attack, Israeli leaders took preemptive action. On June 5, Israeli warplanes struck Egyptian air bases, destroying the bulk of Egypt's air force on the ground and touching off the conflict that would become widely known as the Six-Day War. By June 10, the Israel Defense Forces (IDF) had routed the combined armed forces of Egypt, Syria, and Jordan.

For the Palestinians, Israel's crushing defeat of the Arabs would have profound and long-lasting consequences. Most significantly, Israel after the Six-Day War occupied the Gaza Strip and the West Bank, including East Jerusalem. Although the war produced another flood of refugees—nearly a quarter million Palestinians fled the West Bank—hundreds of thousands remained there and in Gaza. This meant that many Palestinians would be living under Israeli military occupation, a situation that over the long term would lead to much bloodshed on both sides.

Another consequence of the Six-Day War was a change in the attitudes of many Palestinians toward the Arab countries. It was now abundantly clear that Palestinians could not rely on the Arab states to win back Palestine for them; Israel had demonstrated its military superiority. Some Palestinians began contemplating the possibility of settling for a Palestinian state that encompassed the West Bank and Gaza rather than all of traditional Palestine. Others concluded that Palestinians would simply have to take control of the struggle against Israel. In large measure because this had always been Yasir Arafat's message, Arafat and his Fatah faction

Egyptian soldiers examine the wreckage of a downed airplane during the Six-Day War, June 1967. For many Palestinians, Israel's stunning victory against the combined armies of Egypt, Syria, and Jordan ended the illusion that the Arab countries could be counted on to win back their land.

gained control of the PLO—and to a great extent, of the Palestinian national cause. Despite numerous setbacks and the emergence of a number of rival Palestinian groups, Arafat was still the acknowledged leader of the Palestinian people more than 35 years later.

In November 1967 the United Nations attempted to lay the foundations of a diplomatic solution to the Arab-Israeli conflict with the passage of Resolution 242, which essentially called on Israel to withdraw from territories it occupied as the result of the Six-Day War to "secure and recognized boundaries," and required the Arabs to recognize Israel's right to exist and make peace with the Jewish state. The Arab countries and the PLO balked.

The Palestine National Charter, created in July 1968, defined the Palestinian homeland as all of the British Mandate territory and declared, "Armed struggle is the only way to liberate Palestine." Clearly, there was no room for compromise with Israel. But, as Arafat and others recognized, the chances for a conventional military victory over Israel were nil. So Arafat, inspired by revolutions in Cuba, Algeria, and Vietnam, planned to liberate Palestine through a "people's war." At the vanguard of that people's war would be the **fedayeen**, "freedom fighters" from the various Palestinian groups under the PLO umbrella, who would launch guerrilla operations against Israeli targets.

While Arafat's PLO continued to receive military and financial support from Arab countries, including Egypt and Syria, significant friction with the Jordanian government emerged. Jordan was the site not only of many PLO bases but also of the organization's headquarters, which Arafat had moved from East Jerusalem to Amman, the Jordanian capital, in 1968. Gradually the PLO evolved into a

Bitter fighting between the Palestine Liberation Organization and the Jordanian armed forces reduced sections of Amman to rubble in September 1970. Eventually, the PLO was forced from Jordan and moved its headquarters to Beirut, Lebanon.

virtual state-within-a-state inside Jordan. The mere presence of the PLO (whose armed fighters numbered perhaps 15,000) would have been sufficient to concern Jordanian authorities, particularly given the fact that so many Palestinians resided in their country. But by all accounts the PLO brought chaos and lawlessness—ignoring Jordanian sovereignty and harassing and extorting money from local residents, for example. In addition, its guerrilla incursions into Israel prompted Israeli retaliatory bombing of Jordanian villages. Plus, by 1970 Palestinian tactics had grown to include acts of international terrorism. In September, Palestinian radicals (principally from a PLO faction called the Popular Front for the Liberation of Palestine, or PFLP) hijacked three passenger jets—one Swiss, one British, and one American—to Jordan and, after removing the passengers and holding them hostage, blew the airplanes up. Worst of all from the Jordanian point of view, however, some Palestinian leaders began talking openly of overthrowing Jordan's King Hussein, and indeed, an attempt on the king's life was made on September 1.

Finally, Hussein ordered his armed forces to move against the PLO. In 10 days of bitter fighting beginning on September 17, the Jordanian army—despite a brief pro-PLO intervention by Syria—routed Arafat's forces. Hussein and Arafat signed a peace treaty that would have permitted the PLO to remain in Jordan under certain conditions, but the most radical Palestinian groups, including the PFLP, refused to accept the agreement, and Arafat couldn't (or wouldn't) make them. Fighting resumed, and within about a year the PLO had been expelled completely from Jordan.

THE PLO SEIZES THE WORLD STAGE

In the wake of the debacle in Jordan, some observers may have been tempted to write off the PLO and its chairman, Yasir Arafat. But, as writer David Brooks observed in a 2002 *Atlantic Monthly* profile, while Arafat "has proved to be a mediocre guerrilla leader and a terrible administrator [he is] a brilliant image crafter and morale builder." Somehow, amid increasing divisions within the PLO and the emergence of rival Palestinian groups outside it, Arafat managed to, as Brooks puts it, "rally the Palestinian psyche around himself." And, through the use of terrorism, he made it impossible for the world to ignore the Palestinian cause.

The most notorious act of PLO-sponsored terrorism occurred during the 1972 Summer Olympics in Munich, West Germany. In the early-morning hours of September 5, a squad of terrorists from a group calling itself Black September (the name was derived from the PLO-Jordanian war) invaded the dormitory of the Israeli wrestling and weightlifting teams, shot and killed two, and took nine others hostage. A shoot-out at a nearby airfield later in the day claimed the lives of all nine Israeli hostages. Though the shocking attack produced worldwide outrage, as an exercise in publicizing the Palestinian cause it could scarcely have been more successful: an international television audience numbering perhaps in the hundreds of millions saw the unfolding drama, and in the days and weeks that followed, Palestinian issues were examined in many news stories and analyses. (Arafat himself denied any connection with Black September or the Munich massacre, but this claim would later be contradicted.)

Surprisingly, perhaps, the PLO began to gain a measure of political influence and even international respectability by the mid-1970s. Over the objections of Jordan, the Arab League recognized the PLO as the legitimate representative of the Palestinian people and later offered it full membership. The United Nations even granted the PLO observer status.

Meanwhile, Arafat had established his headquarters in Beirut, Lebanon. Like Jordan, Lebanon had a large Palestinian refugee population. And, as previously, chaos followed the PLO in its new

A masked Palestinian terrorist stands on the balcony of a dormitory where his comrades hold nine Israeli athletes hostage during the 1972 Summer Olympics in Munich, West Germany. The notorious incident, in which 11 members of the Israeli Olympic team were killed, publicized the Palestinian cause in a way that was impossible for a horrified world to forget.

home. In fact, the PLO was one of the major participants in the Lebanese civil war, a devastating conflict that broke out in April 1975 and continued, with interruptions, into 1990.

The PLO had long since departed Lebanon by the end of the civil war, however. In June 1982 Israel, responding to cross-border attacks launched against it from southern Lebanon, invaded its neighbor to the north. Israeli troops pushed on to Beirut, trapping the PLO there. But in order to avert a prolonged siege of Lebanon's capital city, the United States pressured Israel to permit the evacuation of the PLO. Arafat and his closest aides moved the organization's headquarters to Tunis, Tunisia, where, for the first time, the chairman was cut off from direct contact with most Palestinians (and, prudently in the eyes of Tunisian officials, from the local population).

PALESTINIANS IN THE OCCUPIED TERRITORIES

While Yasir Arafat and his PLO set about the work of "liberating" Palestine from their headquarters in Beirut and later Tunis, conditions for ordinary Palestinians in the so-called occupied territories—the Israeli–controlled Gaza Strip and West Bank—were changing dramatically. By the late 1970s Israel, under a conservative new Likud Party government, initiated a new settlement policy. Previously, most Israeli settlements in the West Bank had been built near Israel's pre-1967 borders, or away from major Palestinian population centers along strategic points. Now Israeli settlements seemed to crop up everywhere, and in 1984, Israel began a massive

A Palestinian youth with a handful of rocks, Hebron, 1988. During the first *intifada*, images of stone-throwing Palestinians being shot by Israeli soldiers wielding automatic weapons helped win sympathy, throughout much of the world, for the Palestinians in the Israeli-occupied West Bank and Gaza Strip.

road-building project to connect the West Bank settlements directly to Israel, bypassing Palestinian communities. Likud's settlement policy in the West Bank involved various political, social, economic, and even religious factors, but many observers believe that the government's primary goal was to make a future land-for-peace deal with the Palestinians—an arrangement moderate Israelis and Palestinians had begun to contemplate—impossible.

By the mid-1980s, Palestinian officials estimated that Israel claimed up to two-thirds of the occupied territories for settlements, farms, security areas, or roads. In addition to witnessing what they regarded as an Israeli land grab at their expense, many Palestinians resented the daily inconvenience and even humiliation they suffered at the hands of Israeli settlers and the soldiers deployed to protect them. To add to their resentment, an economic slump in the mid-1980s made life even harder for Palestinians.

The simmering resentment boiled over in December 1987, with the beginning of a three-year uprising against Israeli rule in the occupied territories that became known as the ***intifada*** (which in Arabic means "shaking off"). Though the *intifada* included some deadly violence against Israeli settlers and soldiers (along with Palestinians deemed to be collaborators), what much of the world saw was a decidedly one-sided contest, with Israel in the role of harsh oppressor. TV crews captured—almost daily, it seemed—scenes of stone-throwing Palestinian youths being met by Israeli soldiers firing automatic weapons. As the Palestinian casualties mounted (some 700 Palestinians were killed between December 1987 and 1991), worldwide sympathy for the Palestinians grew. Many international observers also condemned Israel's use of a procedure called administrative detention, by which authorities could arrest and jail, essentially for an indefinite period and without criminal charges or trial, any Palestinian deemed a security threat. Because the Israeli authorities could use secret evidence, there was frequently no way for a detainee to know why he or she was being held, much less to mount a legal defense. Thousands of Palestinians were imprisoned in this manner during the *intifada*. And according to Palestinians—and human rights groups such as Amnesty International—conditions for administrative detainees are often harsh. (Israel continues to make use of administrative detention.)

Though the *intifada* ultimately failed to prompt Israel to withdraw from the occupied territories, and though it devastated the local economy, in many ways it marked a turning point in Palestinian history. It united many parts of Palestinian society in the West Bank and Gaza, from intellectuals and professionals to farmers and young street organizers. It marked the first time significant numbers of Palestinians living in the occupied territories, as opposed to the exiled PLO leadership and fedayeen acting in their name, actively opposed Israeli rule. It spurred King Hussein, in 1988, to give up Jordan's claim to the West Bank and recognize Palestine as an independent state. It may also have played a role in convincing more moderate Israeli leaders to entertain a land-for-peace agreement in the West Bank and Gaza. For its part the PLO leadership, at a 1988 meeting of the Palestinian National Council, officially accepted U.N. Resolution 242, recognizing the State of Israel and the United Nations partition of Palestine.

OSLO, THE PALESTINIAN AUTHORITY, AND THE SECOND *INTIFADA*

After Yitzhak Rabin, a former general, became Israel's prime minister in 1992, Israeli and PLO officials conducted secret negotiations in Oslo, Norway. Those talks led to an agreement, dubbed the Oslo accords, by which the PLO officially recognized Israel, Israel recognized the PLO as the legitimate representative of the Palestinian people, and both sides committed to a process designed to lead to a Palestinian state in the West Bank and Gaza Strip. On September 13, 1993, Rabin and Yasir Arafat signed a declaration of principles at a ceremony in Washington, D.C., on the White House lawn.

The Oslo accords envisioned a two-stage process. The first stage, set forth in the Declaration of Principles on Interim Self-Government Arrangements, was to be a five-year period during which the Israeli military would gradually withdraw from areas in the occupied territories and Palestinian self-rule would be established in these **autonomous zones** under the auspices of an interim Palestinian government, called the Palestinian Authority, or PA. The PA and Israeli authorities would cooperate on security and other issues, though Israel would retain overall security control. In

Peace between Israel and the Palestinians, and even the establishment of an independent Palestinian state, seemed within reach when Israeli prime minister Yitzhak Rabin shook hands with PLO chairman Yasir Arafat under the approving eye of President Bill Clinton, September 13, 1993. A decade later, however, the optimism was a distant memory.

Palestinian policemen at a parade in Bethlehem. Under the Oslo accords, Palestinian police in the West Bank and Gaza were supposed to cooperate with Israeli security forces, but mutual suspicion and even direct clashes between the two groups undermined the arrangement.

the second stage of the Oslo peace process, Israel and the PA, having built mutual trust, would enter into final-status negotiations to resolve some of the more contentious issues: the precise nature and boundaries of the Palestinian state, the division of water resources, the fate of Israeli settlements, the status of Jerusalem.

The Oslo accords had many opponents, among Israelis as well as Palestinians. Hard-line Israelis mistrusted Arafat and the PLO and opposed giving up any land in the West Bank. Radical Palestinian **_Islamist_** groups such as Hamas continued to reject Israel's right to exist and threatened to undermine the accords with violence; even among moderate Palestinians who favored a two-state arrangement, many felt Arafat had given away too much.

Nevertheless, when Arafat returned to the West Bank in 1994 from his exile in Tunis, he was greeted with widespread adulation. And in elections held in 1996, Palestinians overwhelmingly elected him *rais* (president or chairman) of the PA (though many international observers took a dim view of the openness of the electoral process).

Meanwhile, implementing the accords and building the trust that the Oslo architects hoped would help lead to a final settlement was proving difficult. In 1995 an Israeli opposed to the peace process assassinated Yitzhak Rabin, Israel's moderate Labor Party prime minister. The following year, Benjamin Netanyahu, a hard-liner from the right-wing Likud Party, became prime minister. Netanyahu had run on a platform opposing the Oslo accords. Under his administration, Israel continued to confiscate land and build settlements in the West Bank, especially around East Jerusalem, which particularly inflamed Palestinian passions. Moreover, the economy of the Palestinian lands was in a terrible state, with little hope for improvement. Israel continued to maintain

Hard-line Likud Party member Benjamin Netanyahu won election as Israel's prime minister in 1996, the year after Yitzhak Rabin's assassination. Netanyahu opposed the Oslo accords, and under his leadership Israeli settlement in the occupied territories was expanded.

control of the natural resources, including water, in the Gaza Strip and the West Bank, limiting economic growth. Repeated border closings because of security reasons meant that many Palestinians couldn't get to their jobs in Israel.

Palestinian violence against Israelis, which had never fully disappeared from the West Bank or Gaza, escalated. Israel charged that the Palestinian Authority was doing little to prevent this violence, and was perhaps even encouraging it. In 1996 Islamist extremists started a campaign of bombings inside Israel proper. In response, Israel closed down borders and enforced curfews in the West Bank and Gaza, which added to Palestinians' hardships and bred more anti-Israel sentiment.

Netanyahu and Arafat—with mediation from U.S. president Bill Clinton—did reach an agreement on certain issues, called the Wye Accord. But the diplomacy stalled until the election, in 1999, of a new Israeli government headed by the Labor Party's Ehud Barak. Barak promoted a revision of the Wye Accord with the PA and in September 1999 committed to reaching a final agreement within a year.

In July 2000, President Clinton invited Barak and Arafat to the presidential retreat at Camp David, Maryland, to negotiate final-status issues as prescribed in the 1993 Oslo accords. At the two-week-long summit, Barak presented Arafat with a proposal for the final borders of a Palestinian state. Arafat rejected Barak's plan without presenting a counterproposal, and the summit concluded with no agreement.

As with so many issues in the Israeli-Palestinian conflict, precisely who is to blame for the failure of the Camp David summit is hotly contested. Most Israelis insist that Barak's proposal was more than generous: some 93 percent of the West Bank and Gaza Strip would have been included in the Palestinian state, and control of Jerusalem would have been divided. Israelis suspect that

In an effort to revive the flagging peace process, Bill Clinton hosted a summit between Yasir Arafat and Israeli prime minister Ehud Barak at the U.S. presidential retreat in Camp David in July 2000. But the summit ended in disarray, and soon afterward the West Bank and Gaza Strip erupted in another violent uprising Palestinians called the Al-Aqsa *intifada*.

Arafat refused to negotiate because he still believed he could pressure Israel into further concessions through more violence. Most Palestinians, on the other hand, vehemently deny that Barak's plan was at all generous. They say that Barak's maps clearly show that the much-touted 93 percent of the land Israel was willing to give up actually consisted of dozens of small islands, surrounded by Israeli settlements and roads policed by Israeli soldiers—hardly a sufficient basis for a viable Palestinian state.

In September 2000 Ariel Sharon, the leader of the Likud Party, visited the area in East Jerusalem that Jews call the Temple Mount, accompanied by hundreds of Israeli riot police. The area contains Judaism's holiest place, the remnants of the Second Temple, destroyed by the Romans in A.D. 70. But what Jews call the Temple Mount is also what Muslims call Al-Haram al-Sharif ("the Noble

Sanctuary"), and it is their religion's third-holiest site, behind only Mecca and Medina. Al-Haram al-Sharif contains two famous mosques, Al-Aqsa and the Dome of the Rock—built over the place where Muhammad is said to have ascended to heaven. Many Palestinians, as well as some international observers, viewed Sharon's visit as a deliberate provocation, and rioting quickly broke out. Within days, the West Bank and Gaza exploded in deadly violence (which many Israelis insist had been planned before Sharon's visit). Palestinians came to call this bloody campaign against Israeli occupation the Al-Aqsa *intifada*.

Largely because of the second *intifada*, Israeli voters elected Ariel Sharon prime minister in February 2001. But the violence only got worse. Increasingly, the Palestinians' weapon of choice became the suicide bomber—a typically young man or woman who detonated explosives attached to his or her body in public places, such as buses and markets, where large numbers of Israelis were present. Responsibility for many of these attacks was claimed by Islamist groups opposed to Arafat's leadership and the peace process in general, including Hamas and the Palestinian Islamic Jihad. For this reason, many Palestinians and their supporters asserted that while Arafat may have wanted to stop the violence, he couldn't. This claim is doubtful, as another group responsible for suicide attacks, the Al-Aqsa Martyrs Brigade, had links to Arafat's Fatah faction—and Arafat's signature was later discovered on documents authorizing payments to the families of suicide bombers.

For his part, Sharon adopted an uncompromising (some would say draconian) policy—and, his critics charged, not simply toward the *intifada*'s leaders and participants, but toward the entire Palestinian population in the West Bank and Gaza. After Palestinian attacks on Israelis, the Israel Defense Forces launched retaliatory raids that, according to a United Nations report, "involved the use of ground troops, attack helicopters, tanks and F-16 fighter jets in civilian areas, including refugee camps, causing significant loss of life among civilians." The families of suicide bombers had their homes bulldozed. Israeli forces assassinated leaders of Palestinian groups deemed responsible for terrorist attacks, sometimes with means that produced civilian casualties. For example, an Israeli rocket fired into an apartment building in

During the Al-Aqsa *intifada*, Islamist terrorist groups opposed to any accommodation with Israel sponsored a string of suicide bombings, some inside Israel itself. Shown here is the aftermath of a Hamas-sponsored attack on a hotel in Netanya during the Jewish holiday of Passover. The bombing, which claimed 20 lives, helped spur a harsh Israeli crackdown in the occupied territories in 2002.

Gaza killed not only the Hamas leader targeted but also 14 others.

After a series of particularly devastating Palestinian suicide bombings around the Jewish holiday of Passover in March 2002, Israeli forces launched Operation Defensive Shield, by which they occupied six of the largest Palestinian cities in the West Bank, including Ramallah (headquarters of the Palestinian Authority), Bethlehem, Nablus, and Jenin. Round-the-clock curfews prevented an estimated 1 million residents of these cities, as well as surrounding towns, villages, and refugee camps, from attending school, going to work, getting food, and obtaining medical treatment. In most cases, these curfews lasted continuously for a week or longer. Thousands of Palestinians were arrested. Fighting between Israel Defense Forces personnel and Palestinian militants, which was particularly intense in Jenin, claimed the lives of nearly 500 Palestinians (according to a U.N. report) and about 25 Israeli soldiers. In addition, about 1,450 Palestinians were wounded, and 17,000 were left homeless or with severely damaged houses.

During Operation Defensive Shield, Israeli forces surrounded the Palestinian Authority's compound in Ramallah, trapping Arafat and many of his top aides inside. In the course of a month-long siege, Israeli tanks and bulldozers destroyed many of the buildings. If, as some analysts believe, the siege was intended to humiliate Arafat, thereby undermining his standing among the Palestinian people and ultimately making way for new Palestinian leadership, it probably backfired. Palestinians seemed to rally behind their embattled leader—with whom Ariel Sharon publicly declared he would never negotiate.

By spring 2003 the two longtime enemies still headed their respective governments, Sharon having won reelection in January. By that time the second *intifada* had claimed the lives of more than 2,000 Palestinians and more than 700 Israelis. Few people on either side of the conflict held out much hope for a quick end to the violence, much less for a lasting peace. The United States (working with Russia, the European Union, and the United Nations) was promoting a "road map" to peace that would establish a Palestinian state in three years—but only if Arafat's power were sharply reduced in favor of a new Palestinian leadership.

labor force is employed in manufacturing, most of these jobs are in small, family-owned businesses that produce low-value items such as soap, cement, and souvenirs for tourists.

By far the largest segment of the Palestinian economy is the service sector, which employs about two-thirds of the workforce and accounts for approximately the same proportion of the country's gross domestic product (GDP)—the total value of goods and services produced annually. Many service-sector workers are employed by the Palestinian Authority (the West Bank and Gaza Strip's largest employer), which, it must be noted, has acquired a reputation for inefficiency and corruption. So another factor in improving the Palestinian economy may be reforming the PA.

THE PLO, THE PA, AND PALESTINIAN POLITICS

In 1993 the Oslo accords and Declaration of Principles led to the establishment of the Palestinian Authority (called the Palestinian National Authority by Palestinians). The PA is not exactly a government but is rather an administrative body that has assumed various governmental duties in the autonomous zones of the West Bank and Gaza Strip.

As the longtime chairman of the Palestine Liberation Organization Executive Committee, Yasir Arafat brought much of the structure and political culture of the PLO to the PA when he assumed control of the West Bank and Gaza administration. Indeed, in order to understand fully the current state of affairs within the PA, it is necessary to examine briefly the history of the PLO.

From the late 1960s to 1996, the PLO and Yasir Arafat were widely seen as the political representatives of the Palestinian people, though this status was never confirmed through an expression of the popular will of Palestinians via democratic elections. From the mid-1970s on, however, the PLO enjoyed diplomatic recognition by the Arab League and the United Nations.

Yasir Arafat leads a vote at a 1987 meeting of the Palestinian National Council. In reality, the PLO's 600-member advisory body held little actual power. Arafat's critics say he brought the inefficient and undemocratic structures of the PLO to the new Palestinian Authority.

However, the PLO was not, and is not, a single, united entity but rather a collection of Palestinian nationalist groups with a wide range of ideologies and differing ideas regarding the shape of a Palestinian state, the role of violence in achieving that state, and, more recently, the possibility of any accommodation with Israel. In the past, Arafat's dominant Fatah faction was unquestionably involved in anti-Israel terrorism. So, too, were many other groups that operated under the PLO umbrella. Indeed, attacks on Israeli civilians formed a primary tactic in the PLO program for the "liberation" of Palestine.

Nonetheless, by the mid-1970s, the PLO had developed the

structure of a government in exile. The PLO was ruled by two bodies, the Palestinian National Council (PNC), which had 600 members and met infrequently, and the Executive Committee, whose members were elected by the PNC and served as Arafat's cabinet. Governed by a national charter known as the Covenant, which denied Israel's right to exist, the PNC had military wings to destroy the Jewish state.

Arafat claims that since the 1970s, the PLO has not been involved in terrorist activity, although experts dismiss that claim. Still, the PLO—or at least Arafat and his Fatah group—seem to have become more pragmatic over the years: the liberation of all of

The Economy of the West Bank and Gaza Strip

Gross domestic product (GDP*): $3.97 billion
GDP per capita: $1,350
Inflation: 1%
Natural resources: arable land
Agriculture (9% of GDP): olives, citrus fruits, vegetables, beef, dairy products (1999 est.)
Industry (28% of GDP): generally small family businesses that produce cement, textiles, soap, and souvenirs for Holy Land tourists (1999 est.)
Services (63% of GDP): security forces, government workers, education (1999 est.)
Foreign trade:
    Imports—$1.9 billion: food, consumer goods, construction materials
    Exports—$603 million: olives, fruit, vegetables, limestone
Currency exchange rate: 4.8230 Israeli shekels = U.S. $1; 0.7096 Jordanian dinars = U.S. $1 (February 2003)

*GDP, or gross domestic product, is the total value of goods and services produced in a country annually.
All figures are 2001 estimates unless otherwise noted.
Sources: World Bank; CIA World Factbook, 2002; Bloomberg.com.

Palestine through armed struggle is no longer seen as a realistic goal, and much of the focus has shifted to establishing an independent state in the West Bank and Gaza through diplomacy—or, cynics would say, through a combination of violence and diplomacy. (It should be noted, however, that some nationalist groups, such as Hamas and the Palestinian Islamic Jihad, reject any accommodation with Israel; they oppose Arafat and have made his task considerably more difficult.)

After signing the Oslo accords, the PLO got rid of the parts of its charter that called for the destruction of Israel. Since the founding of the PA, the PLO has theoretically changed from a "liberation organization" to a "ruling coalition," with the goal of establishing an independent state in agreement with Israel. Under the Oslo accords and according to PA laws, the PLO still has negotiating authority for the Palestinians with the Israeli government.

The first vote for a Palestinian government took place in 1996, when Palestinian residents of the autonomous zones and regions occupied by the Israeli army, as well as East Jerusalem, went to the polls. Although these elections were, in theory, an important step toward creating a democratic government, most independent observers believe that the process fell far short of the standard for free and open elections accepted by Western democracies. For example, in the run-up to the voting, human-rights activists and journalists critical of Arafat were arrested, and the results of primary elections were set aside so that pro-Arafat candidates could appear on the final ballot.

STRUCTURE OF GOVERNMENT

In any event, Arafat won election to the position of *rais* (president or chairman) of the PA. According to the rules of the PA, the executive branch consists of 19 ministries, the heads of which form the cabinet of the *rais*. While the *rais* appoints cabinet members,

In 1996 Palestinians in Gaza and the West Bank went to the polls for the first time to elect Palestinian Authority representatives. In the view of most independent observers, however, the actions of Yasir Arafat and his Fatah associates prevented a free and fair vote.

the legislative branch can veto appointments. Both the executive and legislative branches have the power to create laws.

The Palestinian Authority's legislature is the 88-member Legislative Council. Arafat's Fatah party dominates the council, holding about two-thirds of its seats. Other parties include the Marxist Popular Front for the Liberation of Palestine, the Syrian-backed Democratic Front for the Liberation of Palestine, and the Revolutionary Palestinian Communist Party. Two Islamist parties, Islamic Jihad and Hamas, boycotted the first election. These parties form the major opposition to the PLO. The Legislative Council has limited powers, as no constitution has yet been completed or approved. Also, Israel has the right of veto over economic and

This crowd of Palestinian Muslims was denied access to the Al-Aqsa Mosque for Friday prayers in December 2000, during the early months of the second *intifada*. Palestinians claim that a provocative visit to this area by Israeli politician Ariel Sharon was the spark that ignited the al-Aqsa *intifada*.

security issues. The council cannot govern Jewish settlements, nor does it have the authority to negotiate with Israel.

The judicial branch of the PA has courts run by civilian magistrates for ordinary crimes. There are special security courts for military crimes. Palestinian political prisoners also may be subject to Israeli military courts. Israel maintains courts that are separate from its own legal system for areas of the West Bank occupied by Israel.

The PA security forces include lightly armed police and intelligence units. The role of the security forces has been very contro-versial—and somewhat of a quagmire for Arafat. Israel has demanded that the security forces control and combat Palestinian militants who plan and carry out attacks against Israelis, and the ranks of these militants have only grown since the establishment of the PA as the result of anger and frustration over Israeli settle-ment activities and other divisive issues. In the frequent instances when the Israelis believe that the Palestinian security response to anti-Israel violence has been insufficient, they have carried out their own military strikes in the autonomous zones. This has provoked anger at Arafat's administration among many ordinary Palestinians who bear the brunt of the Israeli incursions. At the same time, however, many analysts believe that Arafat is reluctant to mount a full-scale effort to suppress Palestinian terrorism for fear that the Palestinian groups responsible for that terrorism could destabilize or even overthrow his regime.

Security is not the only problem facing the Palestinian Authority. Critics say that the inefficient institutions of the PLO have been transplanted to the PA. Both the PA and PLO have been criticized for a lack of democratic process and financial corrup-tion. The PA lacks democratic institutions such as a free press and generally does not allow citizens to criticize their government. Human-rights organizations have accused the PA security forces of abusing their powers.

Critics have also pointed out the need for oversight of the PA budget. The PA is largely dependent on international aid, but it has had trouble getting funds from international donors because of its bookkeeping practices. The PA has not been able to demon-strate that funds go toward effective development rather than toward rewarding those close to Arafat. Until the PA has financial institutions that allow donors to see how their money is invested, it probably won't receive the international aid it needs. The PA has made matters worse with its top-heavy bureaucracy. In the late 1990s, the PA had nearly 50,000 employees. Their salaries took up much of the budget, leaving little money for infrastructure improvements.

Because of these and other widespread complaints about Arafat's administration, a younger and more reform-minded Palestinian leadership poised to challenge Arafat's authority seemed to be developing before and in the early days of the Al-Aqsa *intifada*. Both Israeli prime minister Ariel Sharon and U.S. president George W. Bush, in public statements, declared the necessity of a new Palestinian leadership in order to move the peace process forward. Ironically, though, some analysts believe that in laying siege to Arafat's compound in 2002, Sharon undermined the Palestinian opposition, as Palestinians rallied around their embattled *rais*.

RELIGION

The mainstream vision of the future independent Palestinian state includes a secular government. At the same time, the Palestinians are unquestionably a part of the Islamic culture that dominates the Middle East. And, as with the peoples of other countries throughout the region, a minority of Palestinians wants a conservative interpretation of Islam, including *Sharia*, or traditional Islamic law, to be the foundation of their society and government. For groups such as Hamas and the Palestinian Islamic Jihad, the destruction of Israel forms an integral part of their vision for a conservative Muslim society in Palestine. This message has found supporters, particularly among the young and poor who have experienced years of Israeli military occupation in the West Bank and Gaza and who have lost hope for their future. However, most Palestinians tend to be more moderate in their faith; they are among the least conservative of Islamic cultures in the Middle East.

A page from the Qur'an, Islam's holy book. About 90 percent of Palestinians are Sunni Muslims.

More than 90 percent of Arab Palestinians are Muslims (the rate is even higher in Gaza). The vast majority belongs to the Sunni branch of the faith, which is also the dominant branch worldwide.

It is one of the sad ironies of the Palestinian-Israeli conflict that the religions of both cultures have quite a bit in common. Both are monotheistic faiths that place a great emphasis on prayer and ethical conduct. Indeed, Islam even recognizes prophets from the Jewish biblical tradition, such as Abraham (Ibrahim) and Moses (Musa). Stories found in the Jewish Bible also appear in the Islamic holy book, the Qur'an (or Koran).

The essence of Islam is contained in the Five Pillars of Islam, the believer's most important obligations of faith and prayer. *Shahada* is the statement that there is only one God and Muhammad was his last prophet. *Salat* refers to the prayers believers perform five times a day (sunrise, midday, afternoon, sunset, and evening), bowed toward the holy city of Mecca. *Zakat* is the obligation to give a portion of one's income to charity. *Sawm* refers to daytime fasting during the holy month of Ramadan (because the Islamic calendar is based on the lunar cycles, Ramadan occurs in different seasons of the year). The *hajj* is a pilgrimage to Mecca that Muslims, if able, are supposed to make once in their lifetime, during the 12th month of the lunar calendar.

For Muslims, ethical conduct includes behavior that is generous, fair, honest, and respectful, especially in terms of family relations. Islam forbids adultery, gambling, usury, and the consuming of pork or alcohol. The Qur'an, the Hadith (the sayings and teachings of Muhammad), and the Sunna (the example of Muhammad's personal behavior) form a guide to spiritual, ethical, and social behavior for Sunni Muslims.

Fridays are holy days of prayer when people do not work and usually go to the mosque to pray. Any adult male who knows the prayer forms can lead prayers.

Among the non-Muslim religions of Palestinians living in the West Bank and Gaza, Christianity claims the most adherents. About 10 percent of Palestinians are Christians. Many are the descendants of the pre-Islamic Christian communities that dotted the landscape in ancient times. The largest groups of Christians are members of the Eastern Orthodox churches. The Arab Christian Orthodox Patriarchate (Greek rite) of Jerusalem has existed without interruption since the Byzantine era—more than 1,700 years. Among Palestinian communities, there are also Greek Catholic churches and some Roman Catholic churches.

Until recently, the Christian population among Palestinians was disproportionately prosperous because Europeans tended to favor Christians as trade partners during the 19th century. Christians also tended to be better educated than Muslims because they had access to missionary schools set up by Europeans. However, their wealth gave them the opportunity to emigrate after the *Nakba* of 1948. Today, the differences in education and economic status between Christians and Muslims are far less significant.

An elderly Palestinian in Hebron. By the early years of the 21st century, the important West Bank city—located in one of the four hill regions where Palestinian culture developed for many centuries—was home to an estimated 120,000 Palestinians.

The People

Modern Palestinians can be divided into four main groups: those who remained in Israel after 1948 and their descendants; those who live in the Gaza Strip and the West Bank in their own homes and on their own land; refugees from the 1948–49 and 1967 Arab-Israeli wars, living primarily in camps in the West Bank, Gaza, Jordan, Lebanon, and Syria; and those who have settled in other countries, mostly in the Arab world but some as far away as the United States. This last group is called the Palestinian *diaspora*. Precise numbers are hard to come by, but of the roughly 7.5 million Palestinians in the world, about half still reside in historical Palestine—in the West Bank, Gaza, and Israel proper.

SOCIAL ORGANIZATION BEFORE 1948

Before 1948, Palestinians dwelt primarily in the four major hill regions at the center of historical Palestine. Most lived in small villages surrounding the major cities of Jerusalem, Hebron, and Nablus, or in the Galilee region. Up until the 19th century, they were a very indepen-dent peasant people, who often resisted external authority. They lived in family groups called clans, often led by a *sheikh*, and supported themselves by farming small plots of land. Like most residents of the Arab world, the majority of Palestinians followed the values and customs of Islamic civilization, with the exception of the residents of Christian villages.

Over thousands of years, an urban culture developed in the cities of the region. Cities served as manufacturing, crafts, and administrative centers under the Ottoman Empire (and previous rulers). Cities were also religious centers. After the Arab conquest of the mid-600s, important families, called the notables, were the cities' leaders; they were often descendants of the original Islamic conquerors from the Hejaz region, in what is now Saudi Arabia. These people had more power than the village sheikhs. During the Ottoman period, they were part of the imperial administration of the region and competed with one another for power.

In the 19th century, many traditional Palestinian social patterns began to change dramatically. Instead of sheikhs, villages were led by an elected *mukhtar*, or headman. More people moved to the cities, increasing the importance of urban life and accentuating the class separation between urban dwellers and peasants. Wealthy urban families became more westernized as they adopted aspects of European culture and education. In the cities, there were three distinct social classes: the notables; the merchants, traders, and artisans; and the workers. To this day, these three classes continue to mark Palestinian culture.

REFUGEE LIFE

The Arab-Israeli conflict, particularly the wars of 1948–49 and 1967, produced a huge number of Palestinian refugees. In 1998, according to the United Nations Relief Works Agency, a total of 3,573,382 Palestinians were registered as refugees. Among this group, social and economic conditions vary considerably.

A small portion of the Palestinians who fled Palestine, especially during late 1947 and 1948, were members of the urban middle and upper class, and in some cases they managed to take much of their wealth with them. Many of these émigrés gravitated to major cities such as Amman, Jordan; Beirut, Lebanon; and Damascus, Syria. There they tended to adapt fairly readily to their new surroundings, having the financial resources to buy or rent homes and, frequently, the education and business skills to succeed in commercial endeavors. Palestinians from this group contributed significantly to the modernization and development

The People of the Gaza Strip

Population: 1,225,911* (July 2002 est.)
Ethnic groups: Palestinian Arab and other, 99.4%; Jewish, 0.6%
Religions: Muslim (predominantly Sunni), 98.7%; Christian, 0.7%; Jewish, 0.6%
Languages: Arabic, Hebrew (spoken by Israeli settlers and many Palestinians), English (widely understood)
Age structure:
　　0–14 years: 49.7%
　　15–64 years: 47.5%
　　65 years and over: 2.8%
Population growth rate: 3.95%
Birth rate: 41.85 births/1,000 population
Death rate: 4.12 deaths/1,000 population
Infant mortality rate: 24.76 deaths/1,000 live births
Life expectancy at birth:
　　total population: 71.2 years
　　males: 69.95 years
　　females: 72.52 years
Total fertility rate: 6.29 children born/woman
Literacy: figures not available

*Population does not include Israeli settlers in the Gaza Strip (estimated at fewer than 7,000 in August 2001).

All figures are 2002 estimates unless otherwise indicated.
Source: CIA World Factbook, 2002.

The People of the West Bank

Population: 2,163,667* (July 2002 est.)

Ethnic groups: Palestinian Arab and other, 83%; Jewish, 17%

Religions: Muslim, 75% (predominantly Sunni); Jewish, 17%; Christian and other, 8%

Languages: Arabic, Hebrew (spoken by Israeli settlers and many Palestinians), English (widely understood)

Age structure:
  0–14 years: 44.4%
  15–64 years: 52%
  65 years and over: 3.6%

Population growth rate: 3.39%

Birth rate: 34.94 births/1,000 population

Death rate: 4.26 deaths/1,000 population

Infant mortality rate: 21.24 deaths/1,000 live births

Life expectancy at birth:
  total population: 72.47 years
  males: 70.76 years
  females: 74.29 years

Total fertility rate: 4.77 children born/woman

Literacy: figures not available

*Population does not include Israeli settlers in the West Bank (estimated at 182,000 in August 2001) or in East Jerusalem (estimated at 176,000).

All figures are 2002 estimates unless otherwise indicated. Source: CIA World Factbook, 2002.

of countries such as Jordan and the Persian Gulf states. (Nevertheless, Jordan was the only country to offer Palestinians full citizenship.)

Most Palestinian refugees, however, came from the lower classes, and the majority of them ended up in refugee camps. In 1949 the refugee camps—located in Jordan, Lebanon, Syria, and the West Bank and Gaza—began as tent cities, but over the years they evolved into very congested mini-cities with concrete buildings, asphalt roads, and some services, such as running water. They have their own marketplaces, health clinics, and schools.

Often, the traditional social structure of village life was reestablished in the camps. People from the same village tried to live near one another, and they were frequently led by a *mukhtar* from their original village. Even today, many of these Palestinians still identify themselves with the village of their birth, or, if they were born

The Arabic words on the toy rifle brandished by this Palestinian girl read, "We shall return"—an expression of the determination of many refugees to once again live on land lost to Israel in 1948.

after 1948, with their parents' or grandparents' village. Many families displaced in 1948 continue to live in refugee camps and have not merged with the culture of their adopted lands. In their homes, one frequently finds a plaque with the words "Innana 'ai'doun," which means: "We shall return." Despite the passage of more than five decades, during which Israeli military power has eclipsed that of all its Arab enemies combined, many refugees cling to the hope that they will one day reclaim the land that was taken from them in 1948—a fact that has complicated the quest for a workable settlement to the Palestinian-Israeli conflict.

A sense that Israel has perpetrated a grave injustice in taking

Palestinians' land permeates the refugee camps and is one reason these camps have historically been hotbeds of anti-Israel militancy. Another factor is the bleak nature of camp life, where overcrowding, poverty, and unemployment are often widespread. Many camp residents, particularly young people, have little hope for a better future. They frequently question the traditional social structures of Palestinian society, including parental authority, religious obligations, and family solidarity. Under such conditions, many young people are willing to risk their lives to strike a blow against Israel.

In the mid-1990s, there were nearly 60 Palestinian refugee camps: 12 camps in Lebanon, 10 in Syria, 10 in Jordan, 19 in the West Bank, and 8 in Gaza. The poorest and most crowded camps are in Lebanon and Gaza. Since 1994 the refugee camps in the West Bank and Gaza have come under the administration of the Palestinian Authority. Most camp refugees are unskilled laborers or agricultural workers.

Although many Palestinian families have remained in refugee camps since being displaced during the 1948–49 or 1967 wars, many others have moved out. An emphasis on education has proved crucial in this transition. After more than two generations of dispersal, Palestinian exiles have the highest rate of education in the Middle East. Many have flourished economically in the Arab countries where they live, working as business professionals in disproportionate numbers. In particular, rapid economic growth in the Persian Gulf states gave many educated Palestinians of the diaspora opportunities for professional careers and economic security. And in Jordan, where one of the largest communities of diaspora Palestinians lives, a large Palestinian middle and upper class has evolved. They call themselves East Bank Palestinians, and their sense of national identity has been the subject of much debate: among these people there is a range of attitudes about whether Jordan or Palestine is truly home.

WEST BANK AND GAZA PALESTINIANS

The attitudes of the Palestinians in the West Bank are likewise conflicted, but for a different reason. Although the West Bank has a sizable refugee camp population, a large percentage of its residents farm land or live in villages and cities where their families have been for generations. (By contrast, a far-greater proportion of Palestinians living in the Gaza Strip are refugees.) Thus, in a very concrete way, the West Bank is their home. But because of the Israeli military occupation that began in 1967, many West Bank Palestinians report feeling like strangers in their own land. Israel's security requirements—and particularly the protection of Jewish West Bank settlers—invariably trump their rights, Palestinians say. Land confiscations, military checkpoints, curfews, and closures are among the inconveniences and humiliations Palestinians endure regularly. Mortal danger may arise when the Israeli army launches one of its periodic military incursions to root out Palestinian militants.

Gaza's Palestinian population, too, is subject to tough measures by Israeli security forces. But Israeli settlement is not nearly as big an issue in Gaza as in the West Bank (Gaza's settler population stood at fewer than 7,000 in 2001, compared with more than 180,000 in the West Bank). Gaza's population, the majority of whom are refugees, is also less diverse than the population of the West Bank. And while the West Bank has a relatively open border with Jordan, giving it a connection to the outside world, in Gaza, there is no access to any other country except Israel, and that access is carefully restricted. Residents of Gaza are thus quite isolated. They are also much poorer than their counterparts in the West Bank, and their population is younger and growing at a faster rate. Already, the Gaza Strip is one of the most densely populated regions in the world.

THE FORGOTTEN PALESTINIANS: ISRAELI ARABS

While many Palestinians fled the land that became Israel during the *Nakba* of 1948, some remained. Today, these people and their descendants make up approximately 18 percent of Israel's population; the cities where most of them live are East Jerusalem and Nazareth.

Israeli Arabs are an interesting, and isolated, group. They enjoy citizenship rights in Israel but, by some accounts, face suspicion from the majority Jewish population; economically, they are better off than many Palestinians in the diaspora community, but they earn, on average, just 60 percent of what Jewish Israelis earn. At the same time, they are cut off from other Palestinians physically and psychologically—indeed, the society to which they belong is widely viewed as the oppressor of the ethnic group to which they belong. As discussions about the creation of a Palestinian state in Gaza and the West Bank move forward, however uncertainly, the future of this group of Palestinians is even less clear. What would their relationship be to an independent Palestine?

MARRIAGE AND FAMILY LIFE

In spite of the differences among the various groups in the Palestinian population, Palestinian culture shares many features with the rest of the modern Arab world. For most Arabs and most Palestinians, identity and social life center on the family. Households can include a married couple, unmarried children, and other relatives.

In Muslim society, marriage is the foundation for family life. Muslim men may have as many as four wives at a time, but women may have only one husband. Village families are still involved in arranging marriages; even urban people will consult with their families before marrying. For women, having children confers status and security, and the older women of a household have authority over the younger women and children.

Traditional Islamic culture encourages gender separation—that is, it makes a clear distinction between the public world of men and the domestic world of women. Compared with women in some other Arab societies, however, Palestinian women are more integrated into the public world, and many Palestinian women have added public, professional, and political roles to their traditional roles as wives and mothers.

Most Palestinians wear modern Western clothes. However, some women wear scarves and full-length long-sleeved dresses, following Islamic law, which requires them not to expose anything more than their faces, hands, and ankles. During the 1980s more women—even students and workingwomen—began wearing Islamic dress.

Although Palestinians are among the most liberal of Arab Muslims, traditional Islamic culture encourages gender separation. The Palestinian women shown here are dancing at a wedding celebration.

In the Arab world, lunch is the biggest meal of the day and the preferred time for visiting with friends and family. For those whose work prevents them from joining their families at home, fast food, sold at shops and by street vendors, is fresher and more nutritious than American fast food. Much Palestinian food is similar to that of its neighboring countries, and typical ingredients include lamb, yogurt, chicken, bulgur, rice, eggplant, garlic, tomatoes, and flat bread. Flat bread, made from wheat flour, water, and salt but no yeast, is used to scoop up food. Traditional sweets, sold in sweet shops, tend to be sticky and are usually made from nuts, coconut, and spun sugar.

EDUCATION AND CULTURE

In spite of many hardships, the culture of the Palestinian people continues to draw on its ancient traditions, even as it evolves with the modern world. Education has become particularly important for modern Palestinians because it is seen as a key to improving one's life chances. While the elementary and secondary schools in Gaza and the West Bank tend to be underfunded, families encourage their children to graduate and go on to higher education. A university degree is seen as one way to combat poverty and discrimination.

Many educated Palestinians speak English because it is the language of the business world. But all Palestinians speak Arabic, a highly expressive and poetic language. There are two forms of Arabic among the Palestinian population. Written the same in every Arabic country, Modern Standard Arabic is a literary language that evolved from classical Arabic; it has not changed in more than a thousand years because it is the language of the sacred Qur'an. The other form is the Palestinian dialect of Arabic.

Among the arts, literature is probably the most important in Arab culture. The art of writing has been practiced in the Middle East since ancient times; indeed, the alphabet was a Middle

Eastern invention. The modern literature of the Arab world has been inspired by the conflict over Palestine. Palestinian poets and novelists have created a rich literature about the suffering of the displaced Palestinian people. Perhaps the most famous contemporary Palestinian writer is Mamoud Darwish, whose poetry gives voice to the complex blend of strength and anger that is part of modern Palestinian culture.

A Palestinian man prays near Haram al-Khalil (the Tomb of the Patriarchs), Hebron. The site is believed to be the burial place of a figure revered by both Jews and Muslims: the patriarch Abraham or Ibrahim.

Communities

Historical Palestine contained a number of urban communities where the Palestinians lived for centuries. At the end of the Ottoman era, there were ancient cities that were once walled fortresses, like Jerusalem, Acre, Haifa, Jaffa, and Tiberias. There were also many thriving market towns, such as Nablus, Hebron, Beersheba, Gaza, Nazareth, Bethlehem, Jericho, Ashkelon, and Ashdod. Today, many of these old communities are part of Israel. However, several important cities are in the proposed state of Palestine, in the West Bank and the Gaza Strip. Many Palestinians who live there can trace their families' history in those cities back for generations.

HEBRON

The city of Hebron (called "Al-Khalil" in Arabic) is about 22 miles (35 km) south of Jerusalem; the Palestinian Authority estimates that the city and its surrounding communities have a population of about 280,000, making it the largest urban area in the proposed state of Palestine. It is the most important city in the southern half of the West Bank.

Hebron is an ancient city; it was founded by the Canaanites more than 4,000 years ago. In the ancient language of the Canaanites, Hebron means unity.

During the days of the early Islamic empires, Hebron was considered an important cultural hub, and many mosques and centers of learning were built there. Today, Hebron is an important industrial city, with glass manufacturing and leather processing operations. Grapes grown in the surrounding countryside are processed in Hebron to make jam and a kind of molasses.

In a sense, Hebron is emblematic of the tragic history and troubled future of Palestinian-Israeli relations. It contains a site holy to both Jews and Muslims: the Tomb of the Patriarchs. This, according to Jewish tradition, is the burial place of Abraham, the father of the Jewish people; his wife, Sarah; his son Isaac and Isaac's wife, Rebecca; and his grandson Jacob and Jacob's wife, Leah. For Muslims, Abraham is the prophet Ibrahim, and, through Ishmael—a son he had by the servant girl Hagar—he is the father of Muslims. Above the caves where Ibrahim and members of his family are said to be buried is a fortress-like building called Al-Haram. Part of the building, which today houses a mosque, was constructed during the reign of the Jewish king Herod (37–4 B.C.), part during the era of the European Christian crusaders, and part during the Islamic Mamluk Empire. Under the Mamluks, who ruled from Egypt during the 12th century, Jews were forbidden entrance to the tombs. Today, access to the complex is divided between Jews and Muslims.

Hebron was a flashpoint of Arab-Jewish violence during the British Mandate period. In a notorious incident in August 1929, Palestinian mobs, angered by increased Jewish immigration and by reports of Jewish violence against Muslims in Jerusalem, massacred

67 Jewish residents in a days-long rampage. After that and other violence, most of Hebron's 800 or so Jews left the city, and Palestinians took their land.

Since Israel's 1967 occupation of the West Bank, Israelis have reestablished a small but highly divisive presence in Hebron, and the Israeli government has confiscated Arab-owned buildings. By 2003 some 500 Israeli settlers lived in the heart of the Arab Old City, with an additional 7,000 living in settlements on Hebron's outskirts. By contrast, Hebron's Palestinian population was estimated at 120,000.

In recent years, violence perpetrated by both sides has been a frequent occurrence. In the most notorious incident, an Israeli settler named Baruch Goldstein, armed with an automatic rifle, entered the mosque at the Tomb of the Patriarchs and massacred 29 Palestinian Muslims at prayer in 1994. Had such an attack been perpetrated by a Palestinian against Israelis, some Palestinians charged, it would have provoked an Israeli response affecting the whole Palestinian community—military sweeps and large-scale detentions, curfews, closures. But while the Israeli government condemned Goldstein's actions, it treated them as a crime committed by an individual, even though many fellow settlers supported the attack (Goldstein himself was killed during the massacre). And, in an indication of just how wide the gulf between Jewish settlers and Palestinians in Hebron had become, a plaque was erected in honor of Goldstein in the settlement of Kiryat Arba, where the killer had lived. It read: "To the holy Baruch Goldstein, who gave his life for the Jewish people, the Torah and the nation of Israel."

GAZA CITY

With an estimated population of more than 185,000, Gaza City is the largest city in the Gaza Strip. Founded by the Canaanites around 3000 B.C., it is one of the oldest cities in the world. Because of its location between Asia and Africa, Gaza was the scene of many battles between ancient civilizations, including the Egyptians, Assyrians, Persians, Greeks, and Romans. Gaza sits on the dividing line between climates as well, with the desert to the south and the Mediterranean climate to the north.

The ancient city sat on a hill surrounded by a wall with four gates in each direction. A center of trade, its ancient markets were hives of activity, and some of those markets still exist today. In the middle of the 19th century, Gaza was an important trade center, a hub between trade routes from the East to the West. Gaza was a

Gaza residents hoped that the construction of an international airport would improve their economic prospects. But, as shown in this photo, much of the airport was destroyed in December 2001 during an Israeli reprisal for Palestinian suicide bombings.

major grain exporter and an important stop for the hajj caravan from Damascus and points north.

After the growth of the ports of Jaffa and Haifa at the beginning of the 20th century, Gaza's role as a trade center declined. Under Israeli occupation, Gaza could not function as a trading port. Only since 1994, with the limited autonomy of this region, has some port activity resumed. Although efforts have been made to rebuild the port, Israel has restricted growth in the Gaza Strip. Today, Gaza's only trade partners are Israel and Egypt. It imports and exports industrial and agricultural products. Lemons, oranges, and flowers are among the most important agricultural exports. Much of the economy depends on the fishing industry, the products of which are largely exported. Residents hope that the recent construction of an international airport in Gaza will improve the trade situation, but, as with cities and towns in the West Bank, Gaza's economic prospects have been crippled by the second *intifada*.

NABLUS

Nablus is on the site of another ancient city founded by the Canaanites. In the Bible, it is mentioned as the city of Shechem. The current town dates to the Roman era. Located in the northern part of the West Bank, Nablus was an important commercial center and a major stop on the ancient trade routes between the Mediterranean world and the Far East.

Today Nablus has about 160,000 inhabitants, making it the third-largest city in the proposed state of Palestine. It is home to An-Najah University, the largest university in the West Bank.

The Old City of Nablus features narrow, winding lanes, arches, mosques, and many beautiful historic buildings. Restoration projects protect these links to the past. The old market square is still a lively place for shopping, and residents socialize at the many coffeehouses that surround the square. An earthquake in 1927 destroyed many of the city's ancient buildings, and much of Nablus was rebuilt in a more modern style, with well-organized clusters of white-roofed houses graced by ornamental doorways and private courtyards protected from the sun and wind.

In the mountains surrounding Nablus are many olive groves, and during the 19th century, Nablus became an important industrial center for making soap from olive oil. Today, the production of olive oil as a food product continues to be a major industry.

Since 1948 Nablus has been a center for the Palestinian resistance movement against Israel, and a frequent target of Israeli military reprisals. Outside the city are three major refugee camps built in 1948. Home to more than 30,000 Palestinians, they are considered fertile ground for extremist groups such as Hamas.

RAMALLAH

Ramallah, located north of Jerusalem near the geographic center of the West Bank, serves as the headquarters of the Palestinian Authority. With an estimated 2000 population of about 100,000, it is the fourth-largest city in the proposed state of Palestine. From the Aramaic word *Ram* ("hill") and the Arabic word *Allah* ("God"), the city's name thus means "God's Hill." Although historic remains from the Byzantine period and the Crusades era can be found in Ramallah, the current city was founded in the 16th century by Rashed Haddad, a member of a Christian tribe of blacksmiths who came from an area in what is now Jordan. In time, Ramallah became a prosperous agricultural village, differing from surrounding villages only because it was predominantly Christian.

During the 19th century, European Christian missionaries came to this area and founded schools, churches, and hospitals. The town grew into a city during the Mandate period; many beautiful buildings date from this era. Also, the oldest Palestinian university, Birzeit University, was founded in Ramallah in 1924. The city grew

The old and the new: Ramallah. The West Bank city is also the site of the Palestinian Authority's headquarters.

so much that it practically merged with the neighboring town of Al-Bireh. Today, these communities are considered twin cities.

After 1948 Ramallah became home to an influx of refugees from the north and west of Palestine. While the population quickly doubled, more than one-third of the refugees who went to Ramallah eventually immigrated to the United States. The Ramallah community is one of the largest Arab communities in the United States today.

In addition to serving as the administrative headquarters for the PA, Ramallah is one of the West Bank's most important commercial and business centers. A magnet for Palestinians seeking employment and educational opportunities, Ramallah has become one of the West Bank and Gaza's most diverse communities.

JERUSALEM

Jerusalem, with sites sacred to Jews, Muslims, and Christians, is highly disputed ground. Both Israel and the Palestinian

Palestinians at the Damascus Gate in East Jerusalem. The status of East Jerusalem, called the Old City, has long been a source of contention between Israel and the Palestinians.

Authority claim this ancient city as their capital, and the status of Jerusalem has been one of the main stumbling blocks in the Palestinian-Israeli peace process. Today Israel maintains actual control of most of the city, allowing Muslims authority over the 35-acre (14-hectare) Noble Sanctuary area.

Ancient Jerusalem, called the Old City, was divided into four quarters during the many centuries of rule by the Ottoman Empire. The northeast was the Muslim Quarter, the northwest the Christian Quarter, the southeast the Armenian Quarter, and the southwest the Jewish Quarter. After 1948 Jordan occupied East Jerusalem (site of the Old City), while Israel took the newer, western half of the city. As a result of the Six-Day War in June 1967, Israel took the West Bank and East Jerusalem from Jordanian control. Since that time, the city's status has been a point of contention and hostility between the Israeli government and the PLO. Israel has displaced much of the Palestinian population in Jerusalem and, over many objections by the PLO, continued to build settlements, especially outside the wall of the Old City in East Jerusalem. About two-thirds of Jerusalem's estimated 2001 population of 670,000 was Jewish.

At the center of Jerusalem, on elevated ground, is the Noble Sanctuary, which makes up almost one-sixth of the walled Old City. The site contains a mosque completed around A.D. 705, Al-Aqsa (although somewhat confusingly, Palestinians have recently begun referring to the entire Noble Sanctuary as the Al-Aqsa Mosque). Near the center of the Noble Sanctuary is another mosque, the exquisite Dome of the Rock, begun around 685. In Islamic tradition, this is the site where Muhammad ascended to heaven. It is the third most important place of pilgrimage for Muslims, after Mecca and Medina. After 1967 Jordan was given the right to appoint a religious leader to care for the area of the Noble Sanctuary. Today, the Palestinian Authority has assumed that role.

PALESTINIAN FESTIVALS

Among Palestinians, most festivals are celebrations connected to births, weddings, and religious traditions. Special music and dancing also marks plowing, planting, and harvesting in rural areas. Weddings are huge celebrations, showing the great importance of family life in Arab culture. Palestinian village women traditionally make their own wedding dresses, with patterns and embroidered decorations set by their village or clan custom. Before the ceremony, men and women celebrate separately. After the ceremony, feasting, socializing, and dancing can last for several days.

Palestinians also celebrate religious festivals for major saints. These traditional expressions of folk religion mix elements of ancient pre-Islamic faith with Islam. The Nabi Musa (the Prophet Moses) and Nabi Saleh (the Prophet Saleh) festivals are very important. During these celebrations, women prepare special foods, especially sweets. People stay up late into the night socializing, and children enjoy themselves, often taking part in carnival rides set up in the cities. These celebrations create ties among the Palestinians and are unique to Palestinian culture. In the past, these festivals were celebrated after the spring harvest and drew thousands of people from all over Palestine.

Palestinians also celebrate Muslim religious festivals with the rest of the Islamic world. During Ramadan, the month-long Muslim observance of faith, fasting all day ends with a feast after sunset called *iftar*. Special foods, made only during Ramadan, are eaten. After Ramadan ends, there is a three-day celebration called Eid al-Fitr. During this celebration, there is much feasting and socializing; it is common for people to buy new clothes for the occasion. After the hajj, the pilgrimage to Mecca, a similar celebration, Eid al-Adha, is observed. The specific dates of these festivals vary from year to year, as they are determined by the Islamic lunar calendar.

Celebrations and festivals are an important part of Palestinian culture. They not only connect the Palestinians to the larger Islamic world, but also connect Palestinians throughout the world to one another. Hardship and loss have not prevented Palestinian culture from valuing moments of festivity, nor have they caused Palestinians to lose their sense of community during these times of celebration.

Before a model of the Al-Aqsa complex, Palestinians from Yasir Arafat's Fatah faction burn a coffin inscribed with the word *Oslo*—symbolizing both the second *intifada* and the peace accords it killed.

Foreign Relations

Because the Palestinians do not officially control—and have never officially controlled—an independent state, they have no history of conventional foreign relations. Insofar as any single entity can be said to have served as the diplomatic representative of the Palestinians, that entity is the Palestine Liberation Organization. For more than 30 years, the PLO's central goal has, of course, been to establish an independent state for Palestinians. Initially, the state the PLO envisioned encompassed all of Palestine in its British Mandate boundaries, and the destruction of Israel was an explicit aim. Since the 1990s, though, the PLO has apparently accepted the more modest goal of an independent state in the West Bank and Gaza Strip only. Attaining even this scaled-down goal has proved elusive, however, and the United States, Russia, the European Union, and various Arab countries are among the major players in diplomatic efforts to foster the creation of a Palestinian state acceptable to Israel.

LEGACY OF MISTRUST: THE PLO AND ISRAEL

For many years, the PLO and Israel did not regard each other as capable of diplomacy. Before 1978 the two parties held no negotiations except for limited cease-fire agreements, and it wasn't really until the early 1990s that direct, substantive diplomacy began. In a sense, there was nothing for the Palestinians and Israelis to talk about: the PLO was committed to Israel's destruction, and it claimed to be the legitimate representative of all Palestinians, regardless of where they lived. Eventually, events in the Israeli-occupied West Bank and Gaza helped move both parties toward the negotiating table.

By most accounts, when the *intifada* exploded in late 1987, Yasir Arafat and the PLO leadership in Tunis were caught by surprise (though they later insinuated themselves into the uprising). The *intifada* was fueled by rage among West Bank and Gaza Palestinians, and it was directed toward ending the Israeli occupation, not necessarily toward the PLO's grandiose (and thoroughly unrealistic) goal of taking all of Israel. As the uprising continued, Arafat and the PLO, too, evidently settled on the goal of a Palestinian state in the West Bank and Gaza—making negotiation with Israel a possibility.

The *intifada* also helped move many Israeli moderates, including Yitzhak Rabin, toward the idea of negotiating a settlement with the Palestinians. The costs of sustaining the occupation, Rabin and others saw, were simply too great.

Thus began the secret negotiations that led, in 1993, to the Oslo accords. The PLO's affirmation of Israel's right to exist in peace and security, and Israel's recognition of the PLO as the legitimate representative of the Palestinian people, established the foundation for a diplomatic solution to the Palestinian-Israeli conflict.

Yet the road to an independent Palestinian state has been fraught with pitfalls. A decade after Arafat and Rabin shook hands over the Declaration of Principles, the goodwill their agreement engendered has evaporated, and a bitter cycle of violence and retaliation has gripped the West Bank, the Gaza Strip, and Israel proper. In part the breakdown of the peace process may be due to the fact that significant constituencies (and, many people argue, leaders) on both the Palestinian and Israeli sides weren't really prepared to compromise on the difficult issues, consideration of which the Oslo accords postponed for five years, during the intended final-status negotiations. These issues include Israeli settlements in the West Bank and Gaza, water rights, final borders, and the status of Jerusalem and Hebron.

By 2003 Ariel Sharon, Israel's prime minister, had publicly declared his unwillingness to negotiate with Yasir Arafat (accusing Arafat of complicity in terrorism), and his unwillingness to negotiate at all as long as there was any violence against Israelis. In effect, this meant that Palestinian extremists could bypass the Palestinian Authority and dictate the terms of the Israeli-Palestinian agenda. And groups such as Hamas and the Palestinian Islamic Jihad, which oppose the PLO-dominated Palestinian Authority and reject any accommodation with Israel, have claimed responsibility for many suicide bombings and rocket attacks. Many observers worried that as Arafat's appeal among the frustrated, angry, and embattled residents of the Israeli-occupied territories waned, support for these terrorist groups was on the rise.

PALESTINIANS AND THE ARAB COUNTRIES

The creation of an independent Palestinian homeland is a major stated goal of Arab diplomacy, and professions of solidarity with the Palestinian people are virtually required for Arab leaders. Yet relations between the Arab world and Palestinians and the PLO have historically been complex and conflicted.

While Arafat accepted financial support from Arab countries, he resisted attempts by Arab leaders to direct the Palestinian "national struggle." Friction between the PLO and its host nations Jordan and Lebanon ignited into open warfare. (Tunisia's president, Habib Bourguiba, had the prudence to keep Arafat and the PLO leadership largely isolated from his people.)

In 1967 Jordan, which had hundreds of thousands of Palestinians living within its borders and still claimed the West Bank as part of its territory, welcomed the PLO. But as the PLO became more powerful and increasingly flouted the authority of the monarchy, King Hussein was compelled to move against Arafat and his fighters, driving the PLO out of Jordan in the civil war of 1970–71.

Diplomatic relations between Jordan and the PLO remained extremely tense for many years. In 1984 King Hussein permitted a gathering of the Palestinian National Council in Jordan, at which time the king and Arafat reached a joint diplomatic agreement. But PLO-Jordanian relations broke down again the following year after the hijacking of the *Achille Lauro*, an Italian cruise ship, by a terrorist group associated with the PLO. In 1986 Hussein ended negotiations with Arafat because the PLO chairman refused to accept U.N. Resolution 242 by renouncing terrorism against Israel. The relationship between the PLO and Jordan improved dramatically after King Hussein relinquished Jordan's claim to the West Bank in 1988. Since the 1990s, Jordan has played an important role in the peace process, using its friendly relations with the United States and Europe to create dialogue.

Until the late 1970s, the Arab world was uniformly opposed to peace with Israel. But in 1977, Egypt's president, Anwar Sadat, launched a diplomatic initiative that culminated, the following year, in an agreement known as the Camp David Accords—so called because the agreement was hammered out at the U.S. presidential retreat in Camp David, Maryland (with mediation by President Jimmy Carter). The Camp David Accords led to the first Arab-Israeli peace treaty, ratified by Egypt and Israel in 1979. The architects of the accords—Carter, Sadat, and Israeli prime minister Menachem Begin—had hoped that the initiative might produce a wider settlement of the Arab-Israeli conflict, including a self-government arrangement for the Palestinians. But the Arab countries and the Palestinians balked. In fact, the Arab League expelled Egypt for concluding a separate peace with Israel, readmitting its largest member only 10 years later.

Still, a shift in policy with regard to Israel and the Palestinian

When the architects of the Camp David Accords (from left: President Anwar Sadat of Egypt, President Jimmy Carter of the United States, and Prime Minister Menachem Begin of Israel) put their signatures to the document in 1978, they hoped for a broader peace between Israel and the Arabs, including autonomy for Palestinians in the West Bank and Gaza. A quarter century later, their dream still hadn't materialized.

A Palestinian father and his sons walk in the shadow of a wall separating Israeli settlers from Palestinians in Gaza. The lives of future generations of Palestinians and Israelis will be shaped by whether or not these two neighbors can achieve a peaceful resolution to their decades-long conflict—and their success or failure may have important consequences for people in the rest of the world as well.

issue began to take place among many, though not all, Arab countries during the 1980s. In 1982 the Arab summit in Fez, Morocco, produced an agreement stating that the Arab world would recognize Israel in exchange for Palestinian statehood. (This was a new twist on the Israeli position of land for peace: since 1967, it had been Israel's strategy to hold the West Bank and the Golan Heights in exchange for peace with its Arab neighbors.) As countries such as Jordan turned toward diplomacy to resolve their differences with Israel, they put pressure on the PLO to do the same.

Arafat was further pressured to negotiate with Israel in the aftermath of the 1991 Gulf War, which the United States also viewed as a favorable time to reinvigorate the Middle East peace process. In 1990 Iraq's dictator, Saddam Hussein, had launched an invasion of his small southern neighbor, Kuwait. Both are Arab countries. Arafat publicly supported Iraq, alienating wealthy Persian Gulf states, especially Saudi Arabia, that felt threatened by Iraqi aggression. The Gulf states withdrew financial support of the PLO, weakening Arafat's position considerably. After a U.S.-led international coalition convincingly won the Gulf War, expelling the Iraqis from Kuwait, Arafat stood largely isolated within the Arab world.

U.S. AND WESTERN PEACE INITIATIVES

The Madrid conference of 1991, convened at the behest of the United States, brought together representatives of Israel and its Arab neighbors for the purpose of working out their differences. The interests of the PLO, which was not invited, were represented by the Jordanian delegation. Madrid failed to produce breakthroughs, but it did inspire hope for a comprehensive negotiated settlement to the Arab-Israeli conflict.

Two years later, Israeli prime minister Yitzhak Rabin and PLO chairman Yasir Arafat signed the Declaration of Principles of the Oslo accords. Though the signing ceremony was witnessed by President Bill Clinton and took place in Washington, D.C., on the White House lawn, the United States had not actually played a significant role in the negotiations. But Clinton, like presidential predecessors going back to Richard Nixon (1969–74), took an active role in the Middle East peace process. In 1998, for example, he hosted Arafat and Prime Minister Benjamin Netanyahu at the Wye River Conference, designed to facilitate implementation of interim agreements between the Palestinian Authority and Israel, and in 2000 he brought Arafat and Prime Minister Ehud Barak to Camp David for a summit that ultimately failed to rescue the foundering Oslo accords.

Among Palestinians, the United States has been—and continues to be—widely perceived as something less than an impartial mediator. For many years, the United States, like Israel, refused to recognize the PLO's legitimacy as a representative of the Palestinian people. In the early 1980s, for example, President Ronald Reagan tried to establish a peace process in which Jordan would act as the representative of the Palestinians, thereby bypassing the PLO altogether. Moreover, Palestinians point out, the United States refused to pressure Israel into accepting the will of the international community (between 1949 and 1992, Israel's actions were condemned in 69 separate U.N. resolutions). Israel has for years been the recipient of billions of dollars in U.S. military aid, and its military superiority, Palestinians and other Arabs argue, is precisely the reason why Israel has not had to compromise.

Israelis, on the other hand, have since the early 1970s perceived European countries as unfairly pro-Palestinian. Europe depends on oil from the Middle East, and the Arab oil embargo of 1973 underscored the vulnerability of the supply. The desire to placate the oil-producing Arab countries, many Israelis believe, was a significant factor in European support for the PLO. In any event, the European Union has endorsed Palestinian statehood and attempted to use its diplomatic ties with the PLO to continue the peace process.

In the wake of the Al-Aqsa *intifada*, which began in 2000, the United States and the European Union, along with Russia and the United Nations, joined together in a diplomatic initiative to resolve the Palestinian-Israeli conflict. As of early 2003, the Quartet—as these four mediating parties were called—was offering a plan for Palestinian statehood by 2005. The Quartet's plan envisioned a total freeze on new Israeli settlement in the West Bank and Gaza, thereby addressing one of the Palestinians' greatest concerns. It also called for the Palestinians to end violence against Israelis.

Yet it was unclear whether the Quartet's peace plan, or any other, would achieve success in the short term. After winning a convincing reelection victory in January 2003, hard-line Israeli prime minister Ariel Sharon appeared unlikely to negotiate with Arafat, particularly as violence in the West Bank and Gaza continued. Meanwhile Arafat, pressured by Islamist radicals, maintained his tenuous grip on power in the Palestinian Authority.

For the United States, resolving the Israeli-Palestinian conflict had taken on increased importance since the terrorist attacks on New York and Washington, D.C., of September 11, 2001. The Israeli occupation of the West Bank and Gaza Strip was seen as a major contributor to anti-American anger among Arabs. The U.S. presidential administration of George W. Bush hoped that facing down Saddam Hussein, Iraq's dictator, would bring an opportunity to advance the Israeli-Palestinian peace process—but such had been the hope of Bush's father, President George H. W. Bush, more than a decade earlier. As a string of U.S. presidents, international diplomats, Arab heads of state, Israelis, and Palestinians have learned, bringing peace to Palestine is a tall order.

CHRONOLOGY

ca. 8000 B.C.: Earliest known settlement in region at walled city of Jericho.

ca. 1000 B.C.: Establishment of Hebrew kingdom.

ca. 700–300 B.C.: Region conquered, in succession, by Assyrians, Babylonians, and Persians.

ca. 100 B.C.: Romans conquer region.

640: Muslim Arabs conquer region.

Late 11th century: Christian crusaders from Europe invade, conquer important sites in Palestine.

Late 12th century: Arab empire based in Egypt reconquers Palestine.

1516: Ottoman Turks conquer region; Palestine becomes part of the Ottoman Empire.

1830: Egyptian pasha rebels against Ottoman control; claims region of Palestine.

1836: Arabs in Palestine revolt against Egyptian ruler; Ottomans retake region.

1838: British establish consulate in Jerusalem.

ca. 1890: First Zionist settlers purchase land in Palestine region.

1914: World War I begins; Ottoman Empire sides with Germany and Austria-Hungary against Great Britain, France, Russia, and, later, the United States.

1917: Balfour Declaration commits Britain to facilitating the creation of a Jewish homeland in historic Palestine.

1918: World War I ends with the defeat of Ottoman Empire and its allies.

1922: League of Nations approves British Mandate for Palestine; large-scale Jewish immigration begins.

1936–39: Arab Revolt targets the British Mandate authorities and the Zionist movement.

1947: Britain turns Palestine question over to United Nations; U.N. votes to partition Palestine into separate Arab and Jewish states.

1948: In May, Britain withdraws from Palestine, Zionists declare the establishment of the State of Israel, and neighboring states of Syria, Egypt, Jordan, and Lebanon attack Israel, prompting the first Arab-Israeli war.

1949: Arab-Israeli war ends with Israeli victory; Palestinians are left with no homeland.

CHRONOLOGY

1964: Following a conference in Cairo, Egypt, the Palestine Liberation Organization (PLO) is established.

1967: In June, Israel smashes the armed forces of its Arab neighbors in the Six-Day War; as a result, Israel occupies the West Bank and Gaza Strip, home to hundreds of thousands of Palestinians; Yasir Arafat gains control of the PLO.

1968: PLO moves headquarters to Amman, Jordan.

1970–71: PLO and Jordanian army clash; PLO is forced out of Jordan and establishes headquarters in Lebanon.

1979: Egypt and Israel ratify peace treaty stemming from Camp David Accords.

1982: Israel invades Lebanon; PLO is forced to evacuate, settling in Tunisia.

1988–91: The first *intifada*, a revolt against Israeli occupation, takes place in the West Bank and Gaza.

1991: Peace talks in Madrid, Spain, fail to produce Israeli-Palestinian settlement.

1993: Oslo peace accords signed between Israel and the PLO.

1994: Limited Palestinian self-rule implemented in Gaza Strip and West Bank.

1995: New accords call for expansion of Palestinian self-rule to all West Bank cities and villages.

1996: First elections for Palestinian Authority take place; Arafat wins PA presidency.

1998: New accords call for Israeli military withdrawal from more West Bank territory in exchange for stronger Palestinian Authority control of terrorism.

2000: Visit by Israeli politician Ariel Sharon to Noble Sanctuary area of Jerusalem sparks riots, leading to beginning of second (Al-Aqsa) *intifada*.

2001: Ariel Sharon elected prime minister of Israel.

2002: Palestinian suicide bombings increase; Israeli forces invade West Bank towns and cities, destroying homes and arresting thousands of suspected terrorists; Israelis lay siege to PA headquarters in Ramallah for more than a month.

2003: Sharon wins reelection as Israel's prime minister; violence in West Bank and Gaza continues.

GLOSSARY

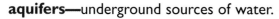

aquifers—underground sources of water.

autonomous zones—regions in the West Bank and the Gaza Strip where, under the Oslo accords, the Palestinian Authority has control.

autonomy—self-government or the right to self-government; independence.

Bedouin—Arabic tribal people from desert regions throughout the Middle East; traditionally, the Bedouin lived in tents and led a nomadic life following their herds.

diaspora—the scattering of a people from their ancestral lands; a community of people living away from their ancestral lands.

fedayeen—Palestinian fighters engaged in guerrilla warfare or terrorism.

ideology—a set of social and political beliefs that motivates a person or group.

intifada—either of two uprisings (beginning in 1987 and 2000) against Israeli military occupation in the West Bank and Gaza Strip.

Islamist—a group or individual promoting the ideals of fundamentalist Islam, including the belief that society and government should be founded on a conservative interpretation of Islamic law.

League of Nations—the forerunner of the United Nations, established after World War I.

legumes—vegetables such as peas and beans whose seeds or seed pods are edible.

mandate—legal authority to govern a land or region, specifically the authority granted by the League of Nations to Great Britain and France to govern the Middle Eastern holdings of the former Ottoman Empire in the wake of World War I.

monotheistic—believing in one God.

mukhtar—a village headman in Arabic culture.

pagan—one who worships many gods, or who has no religious beliefs.

paramilitary—characteristic of a force that is organized along military lines and carries out military operations, but is not an official, national army.

partition—to divide a country or territory into two or more units.

Semitic—belonging to, or descended from, any of a number of ancient peoples of southwestern Asia, including the Phoenicians, Hebrews, and Arabs; also, one of the languages of these peoples.

GLOSSARY

Sharia—Islamic law.

sheikh—a leader in Arabic tribal culture, whose primary role is to resolve disputes or lead his people in battle.

terrorism—the systematic use of terror (for example, through the killing of random civilians) by a group other than a government in order to advance political goals.

Zionism—the movement for a Jewish national homeland in Palestine, which began in the late 19th century and culminated with the establishment of the State of Israel in 1948.

FURTHER READING

Ciment, James. *Palestine/Israel: The Long Conflict.* New York: Facts on File, 1997.

Cohn-Sherbock, Daniel, and Dawoud S. El-Alami. *The Palestine-Israel Conflict: A Beginner's Guide.* New York: Oneworld Publications, 2001.

Farsoun, Samih. *Palestine and the Palestinians.* Boulder, Colo.: Westview Press, 1978.

Hourani, Albert. *A History of the Arab Peoples.* Cambridge, Mass.: Belknap Press of the University of Harvard Press, 1991.

Idinopulos, Thomas A. *Weathered by Miracles: A History of Palestine from Bonaparte and Muhammad Ali to Ben-Gurion and the Mufti.* Chicago: Ivan R. Dee, 1998.

Lewis, Bernard. *The Middle East: A Brief History of the Last 2,000 Years.* New York: Scribner, 1995.

The Middle East. 9th ed. Washington, D.C.: Congressional Quarterly Press, 2000.

Rogan, Eugene L., and Avi Schlaim, eds. *The War for Palestine: Rewriting the History of 1948.* New York: Cambridge University Press, 2001.

Segev, Tom, and Shara Kay, eds. *One Palestine, Complete: Jews and Arabs Under the British Mandate.* New York: Henry Holt, 2000.

Shehadehn, Raja. *Strangers in the House: Coming of Age in Occupied Palestine.* South Royalton, Vt.: Steerforth Press, 1999.

Wallach, John, and Janet Wallach. *Still Small Voices: The Untold Human Stories Behind the Arab-Israeli Conflict in the West Bank and Gaza.* New York: Citadel Press, 1990.

INTERNET RESOURCES

http://www.mideastinfo.com/palestin.htm

Palestinian National Authority website includes links to government, politics, the peace process, non-governmental organizations, education, and news and media, as well as a list of other on-line resources.

http://www.palestine-un.org

The Permanent Observer Mission of Palestine to the United Nations contains information on topography, history, political documents, and current events.

http://ilpalestine.8m.com/holyland/

Includes links to major Palestinian cities, with discussions of the history and culture of these cities.

http://www.cia.gov/cia/publications/factbook/geos/we.html

http://www.cia.gov/cia/publications/factbook/geos/gz.html

The CIA World Factbook sites for the West Bank and Gaza Strip include information on demographics, economics, politics, and more.

http://www.gazelle.8m.net/

Wildlife and environmental issues in the West Bank and Gaza Strip regions.

http://www.palestinehistory.com

Includes an excellent time line with pictures.

http://www.palestine-net.com

Links to culture and heritage sites.

http://www.birzeit.edu/links/

Birzeit University's guide to Palestinian websites has an exhaustive list of links.

http://www.barghouti.com

A culture site that includes good sections on Palestinian folklore and Palestinian literature.

INDEX

Numbers in **bold italic** refer to captions.

INDEX

INDEX

PICTURE CREDITS

CONTRIBUTORS

The **FOREIGN POLICY RESEARCH INSTITUTE (FPRI)** served as editorial consultants for the MODERN MIDDLE EAST NATIONS series. FPRI is one of the nation's oldest "think tanks." The Institute's Middle East Program focuses on Gulf security, monitors the Arab-Israeli peace process, and sponsors an annual conference for teachers on the Middle East, plus periodic briefings on key developments in the region.

Among the FPRI's trustees is a former Secretary of State and a former Secretary of the Navy (and among the FPRI's former trustees and interns, two current Undersecretaries of Defense), not to mention two university presidents emeritus, a foundation president, and several active or retired corporate CEOs.

The scholars of FPRI include a former aide to three U.S. Secretaries of State, a Pulitzer Prize–winning historian, a former president of Swarthmore College and a Bancroft Prize–winning historian, and two former staff members of the National Security Council. And the FPRI counts among its extended network of scholars—especially its Inter-University Study Groups—representatives of diverse disciplines, including political science, history, economics, law, management, religion, sociology, and psychology.

DR. HARVEY SICHERMAN is president and director of the Foreign Policy Research Institute in Philadelphia, Pennsylvania. He has extensive experience in writing, research, and analysis of U.S. foreign and national security policy, both in government and out. He served as Special Assistant to Secretary of State Alexander M. Haig Jr. and as a member of the Policy Planning Staff of Secretary of State James A. Baker III. Dr. Sicherman was also a consultant to Secretary of the Navy John F. Lehman Jr. (1982–1987) and Secretary of State George Shultz (1988).

A graduate of the University of Scranton (B.S., History, 1966), Dr. Sicherman earned his Ph.D. at the University of Pennsylvania (Political Science, 1971), where he received a Salvatori Fellowship. He is author or editor of numerous books and articles, including *America the Vulnerable: Our Military Problems and How to Fix Them* (FPRI, 2002) and *Palestinian Autonomy, Self-Government and Peace* (Westview Press, 1993). He edits *Peacefacts*, an FPRI bulletin that monitors the Arab-Israeli peace process.

ANNA CAREW-MILLER is a freelance writer and former teacher, who lives in northwestern Connecticut with her husband and daughter. Although she has a Ph.D. in American Literature and has done extensive research and writing on literary topics, more recently, Anna has written books for younger readers, including reference books and middle-reader mysteries.